WHO Technical Report Series
967

WHO STUDY GROUP ON TOBACCO PRODUCT REGULATION

Report on the Scientific Basis of Tobacco Product Regulation: Fourth Report of a WHO Study Group

World Health Organization

WHO Library Cataloguing-in-Publication Data

WHO study group on tobacco product regulation : report on the scientific basis of tobacco product regulation : fourth report of a WHO study group.

(WHO Technical report series; 967)

1.Tobacco use disorder - prevention and control. 2.Tobacco industry - legislation. 3.Tobacco control campaigns. 4.Tobacco - chemistry. 5.Metals, Heavy - adverse effects. 6.Metals, Heavy - toxicity. 7.Metals, Heavy - standards. 8.Guidelines. I.World Health Organization. II.WHO Study Group on Tobacco Product Regulation. III.Series.

ISBN 978 92 4 120967 0 (NLM classification: QV 137)

ISSN 0512-3054

Printed in Switzerland

Contents

Participants v

1. **Introduction** 1

2. **Recommendations on toxic elements in tobacco and in cigarette smoke** 3
   - Levels of toxic elements of greatest concern by tobacco type and geographical region 4
   - Research requirements 7
   - Regulatory recommendations 8

3. **Recommendations on the basis for a regulatory framework to reduce the dependence potential of tobacco products** 11
   - Preface 11
   - Background 12
   - Terminology and definitions 14
   - Precedents and experience in regulation of pharmaceutical products 15
   - Dependence potential and product attractiveness and other factors that modulate tobacco product use, risk for dependence and harm 16
   - Challenges in regulating tobacco products as compared with drug products 17
   - Nicotine policy 19
   - Conclusions 21
   - Recommendations for regulatory policy 22
   - Recommendations for research to guide and evaluate regulatory actions and implementation to reduce tobacco product dependence potential 23

4. **Overall recommendations** 25
   - Recommendations on toxic elements in tobacco and in cigarette smoke 25
   - Recommendations on the basis for a regulatory framework to reduce the dependence potential of tobacco products 26

5. **References** 29

Annex 1. Toxic elements in tobacco and in cigarette smoke 37
   - Preface 37
   - Background 37
   - Scope 38
   - Instrumentation commonly used to analyse tobacco and smoke 39
   - Toxic metals in smokeless tobacco products 40
   - Toxic metals in smoked tobacco products 42
   - Selected biological and public health effects of metals 43
   - Summary 67
   - References 69

Participants in the sixth meeting of the WHO Study Group on Tobacco Product Regulation

Buenos Aires, Argentina, 22–24 November 2010

Members

Dr D.L. Ashley, Chief, Emergency Response and Air Toxicants Branch, Centers for Disease Control and Prevention, Atlanta, Georgia, United States of America

Dr O.A. Ayo-Yusuf, Associate Professor, School of Dentistry, University of Pretoria, South Africa

Dr Vera Luiza da Costa e Silva, Independent Consultant, Senior Public Health Specialist, Rio de Janeiro, Brazil

Dr M. Djordjevic, Program Director, National Cancer Institute, Division of Cancer Control and Population Sciences, Tobacco Control Research Branch, Bethesda, Maryland, United States of America

Dr N. Gray, Honorary Senior Associate, Cancer Council Victoria, Melbourne, Australia

Dr S.K. Hammond, Professor of Environmental Health Sciences, School of Public Health, University of California at Berkeley, Berkeley, California, United States of America

Dr J. Henningfield, Professor (Adjunct), Behavioral Biology, The Johns Hopkins University School of Medicine; Vice President, Research, Health Policy, and Abuse Liability Pinney Associates, Bethesda, Maryland, United States of America

Dr A. Opperhuizen, Head, Laboratory for Health Protection Research, National Institute for Public Health and the Environment, Bilthoven, The Netherlands

Dr C. Robertson, Ruth G. and William K. Bowes Professor in the School of Engineering, Department of Chemical Engineering, Stanford University, Stanford, California, United States of America

Dr G. Zaatari (*Chair*), Professor, Department of Pathology and Laboratory Medicine, American University of Beirut, Beirut, Lebanon

WHO secretariat (Tobacco Free Initiative, WHO, Geneva, Switzerland)

Dr D.W. Bettcher, Director

Mr R. Minhas, Technical Officer

Ms E. Tecson, Administrative Assistant

Ms G. Vestal, Technical Officer

1. Introduction

The sixth meeting of the World Health Organization (WHO) Study Group on Tobacco Product Regulation (TobReg) was held in Buenos Aires, Argentina, on 22–24 November 2010. TobReg is mandated to provide the WHO Director-General with scientifically sound, evidence-based recommendations for Member States about tobacco product regulation. In line with the provisions of Articles 9 and 10 of the WHO Framework Convention on Tobacco Control (FCTC), TobReg identifies approaches for regulating tobacco products that pose significant public health issues and raise questions for tobacco control policy.

At its sixth meeting, after reviewing background documents and obtaining clarifications from the presenters, the Study Group discussed heavy metals in tobacco and cigarette smoke, generational and trans-generational tobacco-induced pathogenesis and evidence on epigenetic mechanisms, cigarette butt pollution, a novel environmental approach to reducing tobacco consumption and the rationale for a regulatory framework to reduce the dependence potential of tobacco products.

Regulation of tobacco products is essential for tobacco control and is endorsed by the WHO FCTC in provisions of its Articles 9, 10 and 11. Regulation serves public health goals by meaningful surveillance of the manufacture, packaging, labelling and distribution of tobacco products. Scientifically based principles for implementing the articles create synergy and mutual reinforcement of the regulatory practices described in each article.

Tobacco product regulation includes regulating their contents and emissions by testing, measuring and mandating disclosure of the results, and regulating their packaging and labelling. Government supervision is required for manufacture and for enforcement of regulations on the design, contents and emissions of tobacco products, as well as their distribution, packaging and labelling, with the aim of protecting and promoting public health.

Chemical consumer products are usually regulated after a review of the scientific evidence on the hazards associated with the product, the exposure likely to occur, the patterns of use and the marketing messages of the manufacturer.

Many jurisdictions require manufacturers to classify and label products according to their hazardous properties, to control the hazardous contents or to limit the advertising, promotion and sponsorship of such products.

TobReg reviews the scientific evidence on topics related to tobacco product regulation and identifies the research needed to fill regulatory gaps in tobacco control. The Study Group is composed of national and international scientific experts on product regulation, treatment of tobacco dependence and laboratory analysis of tobacco ingredients and emissions. As a formalized entity of WHO, the Study Group reports to the WHO Executive Board through the Director-General to draw the attention of Member States to the Organization's work in tobacco product regulation, which is a complex area of tobacco control.

This report presents the conclusions and recommendations of the Study Group at its sixth meeting on toxic elements in tobacco and in cigarette smoke and on the basis for a regulatory framework to reduce the dependence potential of tobacco products. The following two sections present the recommendations, and the overall recommendations are summarized in section 4. This volume also includes the full background document that served as the basis for TobReg's deliberations on heavy metals.

The Study Group hopes that the recommendations contained in this report, as well as its other recommendations and advisory notes, will be useful to countries in implementing the product regulation provisions of the WHO FCTC.

2. Recommendations on toxic elements in tobacco and in cigarette smoke

This advisory is based on a comprehensive review provided as a background paper (Annex 1). Heavy metals are found in tobacco leaf, processed tobacco (both cigarettes and smokeless tobacco) as well as tobacco smoke and smokeless tobacco emissions. These metals are absorbed from the soil, occur in air pollution and derive from agricultural treatments during tobacco growing, curing and processing. The amounts of the metals in tobacco products vary widely, depending on the geographical location in which the tobacco leaf is grown.

Much of the evidence for the toxicity of individual metals comes from studies of occupational exposure to levels much higher than those that are likely to occur from tobacco use. The biological effects of metals with carcinogenic and other toxic effects delivered directly to the lung or oral mucosa is, however, of concern, especially when they are delivered in combination with other known carcinogens, sensitizers (such as polycyclic aromatic hydrocarbons, nickel, cobalt and some forms of chromium) and toxicants in smoke. These factors may contribute to the differences in disease risks associated with different tobacco products and with the same type of tobacco product in different geographical regions.

The exposures of concern for human toxicity depend on the metal, as some are acutely toxic and are cleared by the body, whereas others accumulate over time and may become increasingly toxic with increasing duration of exposure. Still others may sensitize various organ systems to the actions of other tobacco or non-tobacco toxicants and allergens. Some metals found in tobacco are essential human nutrients, including iron, copper, chromium and manganese, but high levels of these elements in certain organ systems may contribute to injury in some people.

Among the metals identified in tobacco products that have been shown to be carcinogenic are arsenic, cadmium, lead, nickel and the radioactive substances polonium-210 and lead-210 (*1*). Arsenic, cadmium and nickel can cause lung injury. Cadmium and lead are of particular concern because of their long-term storage in the body. Other concerns include the capacity of some metals to sensitize tissues to immune response, cellular injury and tissue repair processes.

Metals to which smokers have been shown to be more highly exposed than nonsmokers include aluminium, arsenic, cadmium and lead.

Levels of toxic elements of greatest concern by tobacco product type and geographical region

Arsenic

Arsenic concentrations of 0.13–0.29 µg/g dried tobacco were found in popular brands of moist snuff sold in the United States, and a mean of 0.19 µg/g tobacco was reported in 17 samples of leaf tobacco sold for chewing (*2*). Arsenic concentrations of 0.143–0.437 µg/g were found in popular brands of smokeless tobacco available on the Canadian market (*3*). Concentrations of 0.1–1.2 µg/g arsenic were found in samples of Indian chewing tobacco (*4*) and 0.11–3.5 µg/g in a variety of Indian smokeless tobacco products (*5*). Local Ghanaian snuff contained 0.108–0.256 µg/g arsenic (*6*).

Arsenic has been reported to be present in tobacco at mean concentrations of 0.151 µg/g tobacco in Canadian domestic cigarettes (*7*) and 0.73–0.86 µg/g tobacco mass in cigarettes in Pakistan (*8*). Arsenic concentrations of 0.250 µg/g tobacco were measured in two domestic United States cigarette brands and 0.370–1.07 µg/g tobacco in three corresponding counterfeits (*9*). Arsenic concentrations of < 0.1–0.7 µg/g were reported in tobacco from legally purchased cigarettes in the United Kingdom and < 0.1–2.1 µg/g in tobacco from corresponding counterfeit cigarettes (*10*).

The mean arsenic levels in smoke delivered from 48 Philip Morris USA and Philip Morris International commercial and exploratory brands were found to be from 'below detection limit' to 0.0055 µg/cigarette with the International Standards Organization (ISO) smoking regimen and from 'below detection limit' to 0.0145 µg/cigarette with the Health Canada Intense regimen (*11*).

Cadmium

Cadmium was found at mean concentrations of 0.66–1.88 µg/g dried tobacco in popular brands of moist snuff sold in the United States and 1.44 µg/g tobacco in 17 samples of leaf tobacco sold for chewing (*2*), while concentrations of 0.73–1.58 µg/g dried tobacco were found in eight brands of moist and dry snuff (*12*). Cadmium concentrations of 0.300–1.086 µg/g tobacco were found in popular brands of smokeless tobacco available on the Canadian market (*3*). Concentrations of 0.3–1.5 µg/g cadmium were reported in samples of Indian chewing tobacco (*4*) and 0.1–3.1 µg/g in a variety of Indian smokeless tobacco products (*5*); Verma et al. (*13*) reported 0.25–0.60 µg/g mean cadmium concentrations in snuff and chewing tobacco in India. Concentrations of 1.056–1.105 µg/g cadmium were measured in local Ghanaian snuff (*6*).

The extractable cadmium concentrations in artificial saliva were 0.302–0.342 µg/g dried tobacco for five popular brands of moist snuff sold in the United States (21–47% of total) and a mean of 0.351–0.508 µg/g (23–30% of total) for three samples of leaf tobacco sold for chewing (*2*).

Cadmium has been reported to be present at a mean concentration of 0.930 µg/g tobacco in Canadian domestic cigarettes (*7*) and 2.2–4.5 µg/g tobacco mass in cigarettes in Pakistan (*8*). Cadmium concentrations of 0.5–0.8 µg/g were reported in tobacco from legally purchased cigarettes in the United Kingdom and < 0.2–6.1 µg/g in tobacco from corresponding counterfeit cigarettes (*10*). Mean concentrations of 0.28–0.87 µg/g cadmium were found in tobacco from cigarettes available in India (*13*).

The mean concentrations of cadmium in cigarette smoke particulate matter generated by the ISO smoking regimen from cigarettes available in the United States in 2002 were 0.0138–0.0183 µg/cigarette (ultralight), 0.0184–0.0324 µg/cigarette (light) and 0.0384–0.0624 µg/cigarette (full flavour) (*14*). The mean deliveries of cadmium in smoke from 48 Philip Morris USA and Philip Morris International commercial and exploratory brands were 0.0016–0.101 µg/cigarette with the ISO smoking regimen and 0.0435–0.1971 µg/cigarette with the Health Canada Intense regimen (*11*). The mean delivery of cadmium in smoke generated by the ISO smoking regimen from 247 cigarette brands in Canada in 2004, including 15 imported brands, was 0.0576 µg/domestic cigarette and 0.0523 µg/imported cigarette. With the Health Canada Intense regimen, the reported mean cadmium delivery was 0.1608 µg/domestic cigarette and 0.1571 µg/imported cigarette (*7*).

Lead

Mean lead concentrations of 0.28–0.85 µg/g dried tobacco were reported in popular brands of moist snuff sold in the United States and a mean of 0.55 µg/g tobacco in 17 samples of leaf tobacco sold for chewing (*2*), while levels of 0.27–2.96 µg/g dried tobacco were found in eight brands of moist and dry snuff available at that time (*12*). Lead concentrations of 0.233–1.202 µg/g were found in popular brands of smokeless tobacco available on the Canadian market (*3*). Concentrations of 0.03–33.3 µg/g lead were found in a variety of Indian smokeless tobacco products (*5*), and 1.76–13 µg/g mean lead concentrations were found in snuff and chewing tobacco available in India (*13*).

The extractable lead concentration in artificial saliva for Kentucky reference moist snuff tobacco 1S3 was 0.153 µg/g dried tobacco (8.0% of total). The concentrations of other extractable materials were < 0.13 µg/g (*2*).

Lead has been reported at mean concentrations of 0.257 µg/g tobacco from Canadian domestic cigarettes (*7*) and 1.1–1.6 µg/g tobacco mass in cigarettes in Pakistan (*8*). Lead concentrations of 0.604 and 0.607 µg/g tobacco were reported in two domestic United States cigarette brands and 4.54–7.93 µg/g tobacco in three corresponding counterfeits (*9*). Lead concentrations of 0.4–0.9 µg/g were reported in tobacco from legally purchased cigarettes in the United Kingdom and < 0.1–10.3 µg/g in tobacco from corresponding counterfeit cigarettes (*10*). The mean lead concentrations in tobacco from cigarettes available in India were 0.79–5.79 µg/g (*13*).

The mean concentrations of lead in cigarette smoke particulate matter generated with the ISO smoking regimen from domestic brands purchased in the United States in 2002 were < 0.0071–0.0075 µg/cigarette (ultralight), 0.0096–0.0172 µg/cigarette (light) and 0.0166–0.0289 µg/cigarette (full flavour) (*14*). The mean lead deliveries in smoke from 48 Philip Morris USA and Philip Morris International commercial and exploratory brands were 0.0039–0.0392 µg/cigarette with the ISO smoking regimen and 0.0257–0.0932 µg/cigarette with the Health Canada Intense regimen (*11*). The mean lead deliveries in smoke from 247 cigarette brands obtained in Canada in 2004, including 15 imported brands, were 0.0167 µg/domestic cigarette and 0.0113 µg/imported cigarette with the ISO smoking regimen and 0.0372 µg/domestic cigarette and 0.0342 µg/imported cigarette with the Health Canada Intense regimen (*7*).

Nickel

Mean nickel concentrations of 1.39–2.73 µg/g dried tobacco were reported in popular brands of moist snuff sold in the United States and a mean of 2.32 µg/g tobacco in 17 samples of leaf tobacco sold for chewing (*2*). Nickel concentrations of 0.844–2.045 µg/g were found in popular brands of smokeless tobacco available on the Canadian market (*3*). The mean nickel concentrations in snuff and chewing tobacco available in India were 1.33–13.05 µg/g (*13*).

The extractable nickel concentrations in artificial saliva were 0.554–1.153 µg/g dried tobacco for five popular brands of moist snuff sold in the United States (31–46% of total) and a mean of 0.370–0.739 µg/g (30–40% of total) for three samples of chewing tobacco (*2*).

Nickel has been reported to be present at a mean concentration of 0.250 µg/g tobacco from Canadian domestic cigarettes (*7*) and at mean concentrations of 1.2–1.8 µg/g tobacco mass in cigarettes from Pakistan (*8*). Nickel concentrations of 1.132 and 1.180 µg/g tobacco were found in two domestic United States cigarette brands and 0.358–0.554 µg/g tobacco in three corresponding counterfeits (*9*). Nickel concentrations of 1.1–2.7 µg/g were reported in tobacco from legally purchased cigarettes available in the United Kingdom and 0.9–9.2 µg/g in tobacco filler from counterfeit cigarettes (*10*). The mean nickel concentrations in tobacco from cigarettes available in India were 7.21–10.24 µg/g (*13*).

Polonium-210 and lead-210

Activities of 0.16–0.64 pCi/g (5.9–24 mBq/g) polonium-210 were measured in dried tobacco from eight brands of moist and dry snuff available in the United States in 1987 (*12*). A mean extractable polonium-210 activity in human saliva of 8.7–13.9 mBq/g dried tobacco and a mean extractable lead-210 activity of 8.6–11.6 mBq/g dried tobacco were reported for six brands of moist snuff sold in the United States (*15*).

A mean polonium-210 activity of 10.9–27.4 mBq/g and a lead-210 activity of 11.9–30.2 mBq/g were reported in Brazilian cigarette tobacco (*16*). Lead-210 activity was found to be 6.3–18.2 mBq/g in Greek tobacco (*17*), while a mean polonium-210 activity of 3.6–17.0 mBq/g and a mean lead-210 activity of 7.3–16.7 mBq/g were found in Greek cigarette tobacco filler (*18*). Mean activities of 6.84–17.49 mBq/cigarette were reported for polonium-210 in Italian cigarette brands, including some imports (*19*), and a mean polonium-210 activity of 18–29 mBq/g and a mean lead-210 activity of 17–24 mBq/g were found in Chinese cigarette tobacco (*20*).

Schayer et al. (*20*) reported transfer of polonium-210 and lead-210 from two Chinese cigarettes into smoke and an estimated mean intake (based on smoking 20 cigarettes/day) of 1.85 mBq/cigarette of lead-210 and 3.0 mBq/cigarette of polonium-210. Cigarette smoking in China may therefore be a major source of people's daily intake of lead-210 and polonium-210.

Research requirements

- Further studies are required on the concentrations of metals in smokeless tobacco, smokeless tobacco additives and smoked tobacco products, including cigarette tobacco, cigars, pipes, rolling tobacco and waterpipe tobacco, produced in all geographical regions. Results should be acquired with standardized methods, certified standards and certified or standard reference materials, such as tobacco and other leaf reference materials, to assure the reproducibility and accuracy of data.

- Further studies are required on the concentrations of metals in tobacco smoke obtained with the ISO and Intense regimens in order to maintain current knowledge on the physical transport of metals into smoke.
- Studies in experimental animals are needed on the cumulative effects of long-term inhalation of fine and ultrafine particulate containing neurotoxic metal ions at concentrations similar to those delivered in cigarette smoke (individually and combined). Studies should be conducted on the interactions among aluminium, cadmium, lead, copper, iron, manganese and zinc in the brain.
- Studies are required on the possible relations among metals in smokeless tobacco in producing or exacerbating lesions of the oral mucosa and submucosa. Studies should be conducted on cumulative concentrations of metals in oral epithelial cells as a consequence of smokeless tobacco use.
- Biomonitoring should be conducted to measure the rates of systemic absorption, distribution, metabolism and clearance of metals in smokeless tobacco.
- The rates of systemic absorption, distribution, metabolism and clearance of metals in smokeless tobacco used in different geographical regions should be compared.
- Further studies are needed of the relations between inhalation of metal ions (alone and in combination with other smoke constituents that sensitize the lung) and chronic obstructive and interstitial lung disease.
- Studies should be conducted on the etiological role of the metals in second-hand smoke and the prevalence of asthma in children.
- Studies are needed on the relation between manganese oxidation state, chromium oxidation state and lung pathophysiology.
- Studies should be conducted to define the agricultural practices necessary to minimize absorption of metals from soil, including appropriate control of pH and phosphate fertilizers.
- Appropriate standards, reference tobacco products and appropriate examples of commercial products to be used for comparison should be developed, made available and used in studies. The methods and standards used should be reported in all publications to account for the variations in tobacco products in different geographical areas.

Regulatory recommendations

- Regulatory authorities should consider requiring manufacturers to test cured tobacco purchased from each new agricultural source for levels of arsenic, cadmium, lead and nickel. The results of testing should be reported to regulatory authorities and verified by those authorities as appropriate.

- Regulatory authorities should consider monitoring the tobacco blends in both combustible and noncombustible products offered for sale by requiring testing for levels of arsenic, cadmium, lead and nickel by brand periodically and whenever the source of the tobacco shows substantial increases in the concentrations of any of the metals tested. The results of testing by manufacturers should be reported to regulatory authorities and verified by those authorities as appropriate.
- When the levels of metals found in different brands of the same tobacco product vary widely, regulatory authorities might consider establishing limits on concentrations or take other actions to limit human exposure.

3. Recommendations on the basis for a regulatory framework to reduce the dependence potential of tobacco products

Preface

This scientific advisory addresses the rationale for a regulatory framework for reducing the dependence ('addiction') potential of tobacco products. These recommendations specifically address Article 9 of the FCTC:

> *Regulation of the contents of tobacco products*
> The Conference of the Parties, in consultation with competent international bodies, shall propose guidelines for testing and measuring the contents and emissions of tobacco products, and for the regulation of these contents and emissions. Each Party shall, where approved by competent national authorities, adopt and implement effective legislative, executive and administrative or other measures for such testing and measuring, and for such regulation.

The advisory will also comply with Article 14, which is intended to reduce tobacco product demand by more effective prevention and cessation initiatives.

These recommendations were made because tobacco companies design and manufacture their products to increase their dependence potential and attractiveness; the intent of the companies is to increase tobacco product use and dependence by undermining prevention, cessation and tobacco control measures (*21–25*). A regulatory framework designed to reduce the dependence potential and attractiveness of tobacco products could improve public health, as it would strengthen tobacco control initiatives to reduce the prevalence of tobacco use and the resulting morbidity and mortality.

Policy-makers and regulatory agencies in States Parties to the WHO FCTC have increasingly sought guidance from WHO on the scientific foundation of and potential approaches to a regulatory framework for reducing the dependence potential of tobacco products. This scientific advisory is intended to provide a basis for further discussion and the development of a regulatory framework. The specific purpose of regulating dependence potential is to reduce the prevalence of tobacco use and harm by reducing the risk and severity of dependence as a biological force that contributes to the perpetuation of tobacco use.

Background

The basis of a regulatory framework for reducing tobacco product dependence potential is scientific understanding of the determinants and evidence that the design and manufacture of tobacco products can increase or decrease dependence potential. The primary dependence-producing drug in tobacco is nicotine, and the way in which nicotine is delivered to the user through tobacco maximizes its dependence potential (*22,26*). Several decades of research have shown that the dependence-producing effects of nicotine are directly influenced by the dose and speed of delivery and by associated sensory and environmental stimuli (*26–28*). Many of the design features of tobacco products can be controlled, such as nicotine content, tobacco pH, smoke particle size and other factors that can affect the speed of nicotine release and absorption. Additionally, other contents and nicotine metabolites, including anabasine, nornicotine and monoamine oxidase-inhibiting substances, could add to the dependence potential of the products (*29–31*).

Experience with pharmaceutical nicotine and other drug delivery systems (e.g. for delivering opioids, stimulants and cannabinoids) has demonstrated that dependence potential can be altered by the design and contents of the product (*32–35*). In the case of prescription pharmaceuticals, regulatory frameworks function to reduce dependence potential by predicating approval on both the dependence potential and other possible harmful effects. Decisions regarding drug approval include restrictions to limit access and marketing if the drug is approved (*36*). This gives a powerful incentive to drug manufacturers to design and market their drugs so as to minimize abuse, dependence and use by unintended populations (*33,37–39*). Drugs with design features that contribute unnecessarily to dependence potential may be denied approval by regulatory agencies or approved with controls, including post-marketing restrictions intended to mitigate risks and to detect them should they occur. (For discussion and examples, see *38–42*.)

The release of millions of previously secret tobacco industry documents in the 1990s revealed that the tobacco industry did much more than manufacture and sell inherently addictive tobacco products. It is now clear that the industry actively investigated the effects of nicotine and other substances on the nervous system in an effort to increase the addictiveness (hereafter referred to by the more technically acceptable term 'dependence potential') of their products (*21–25*). For example, the British American Tobacco company was exploring the neurophysiological effects of nicotine in the 1950s (*24,43*). The first successful rodent model of nicotine self-administration was developed by Philip Morris in about 1981. The results raised such critical issues that Philip Morris closed the laboratory and acted to prevent dissemination of its findings when its legal counsel became aware of the research (*44–46*). These studies were only the tip of the tobacco research 'iceberg'—the industry's work in designing increasingly more dependence-producing products. Tobacco litigation and investigations by the United States Food and Drug Administration and WHO unveiled decades of such industry research (*21,24,25,43,47–51*).

The approaches used by the tobacco industry included manipulation of the nicotine dosing capacity of its products, products designed to increase the speed of nicotine delivery and hence its addictive 'impact' or 'kick', control of tobacco and smoke pH to increase the unprotonated ('free base') fraction of nicotine in the smoke, control of smoke particle size to increase lung penetration efficiency, product engineering to increase stimulation of the trigeminal nerves of the oral cavity and upper airways, and the use of a broad range of chemical additives to make smoke feel smoother, cooler and more pleasant, in order to facilitate deep inhalation and the transition to addiction (*35,43,50–55*). These approaches to increase tobacco dependence potential are targets for regulation that could be used within a regulatory framework, in which limits are set or the changes in the product are reversed.

In apparent coordination with product designs intended to increase dependence potential, design has also been used to increase the attractiveness of the products to target populations. These included 'starter' smokeless tobacco products, with a lower nicotine delivery than maintenance products but flavoured, packaged and marketed to be more attractive to young people (*25,30*). Other initiatives have been the design, packaging and marketing of cigarettes to be particularly attractive to certain populations in many countries on the basis of gender, socioeconomic status and racial or ethnic affiliation. They include cigarettes designed to promote the illusion that they are less harmful to health. Increasing the attractiveness and appeal of a product to a target population can involve adding flavour and smell, the use of colours and graphics on the product and packaging, express or implicit claims, and a broad range of additional marketing tools. These are beyond the scope of this report, but many aspects have been addressed elsewhere (*25,30,56*).

At its fourth session, the Conference of the Parties to the FCTC accepted the goal of "reducing tobacco-attributable disease and premature death by reducing the attractiveness of tobacco products, reducing their addictiveness (or dependence liability) or reducing their overall toxicity" (*57*). These three aspects of product regulation can be addressed in various ways, according to the requirements of different countries. The Parties to the FCTC differ in the approaches they will take in the near term; for example, Canada has banned selected additives, such as most flavouring preparations, from cigarettes and little cigars, to help reduce their attractiveness (*58*).

Regulatory action can be taken now, because scientific knowledge about tobacco products and about regulatory measures to control the dependence potential of pharmaceutical products has been increasing rapidly since the 1990s. Precedents for a regulatory framework include national and international initiatives to control drug abuse and dependence by regulation. These precedents include aspects of drug control that are applicable to tobacco product regulation, while other aspects would appear not to be feasible or appropriate. As discussed below, tobacco products pose complex challenges that may be more difficult to address than those posed by regulated drug products.

This advisory includes conclusions that can guide regulatory policy for a framework to reduce the dependence potential of tobacco products. It is an extension of earlier recommendations of the Scientific Advisory Committee on Tobacco Product Regulation and TobReg documents and is designed to provide a foundation for regulation to advance tobacco control in general (*25*, *59–63*). Specifically, it extends the earlier WHO TobReg advisory on reducing dependence potential and the attractiveness of tobacco products (*25*).

Terminology and definitions

Dependence potential: the term preferred by the WHO Expert Committee on Drug Dependence; often used interchangeably with 'addictiveness', used by the Scientific Committee on Emerging and Newly Identified Health Risks, 'abuse liability', generally used by the College on Problems of Drug Dependence, and 'abuse potential' (*30,42,64*); refers to the pharmacological properties of a drug that can lead to abuse and dependence

Abuse liability: the operational term used by the WHO Expert Committee on Drug Dependence to assess the pharmacologically determined risk for abuse and dependence

Attractiveness or *appeal* of products to potential and current consumers: often referred to as 'consumer appeal', 'product appeal' or 'product attractiveness'. It is related to many factors, including product design features, the sensory characteristics of products such as taste and smell, advertising and promotion, image, cost, the targeted population, positioning among other products and claims for benefits and risks (*56,65–68*).

Precedents and experience in the regulation of pharmaceutical products

Regulation of manufactured products on the basis of their dependence potential is not a new concept but has been a systematic approach of medicines regulatory agencies worldwide and by WHO since at least the 1960s. For example, the WHO Expert Committee on Drug Dependence evaluates dependence potential on the basis of scientific evidence from laboratory and epidemiological studies in order to regulate drugs in accordance with three international drug control treaties: the 1961 Single Convention on Narcotic Drugs, which addressed opium-, coca- and marijuana-based substances; the 1971 Convention on Psychotropic Substances; and the 1988 Convention against Illicit Traffic in Narcotic Drugs and Psychotropic Substances (*36,42*). These treaties exempt tobacco, and it is not recommended in this advisory that tobacco should be subject to such regulation. If tobacco products were regulated on the basis of these treaties, they would have to be either banned or exempted, because most if not all meet the criteria for high dependence potential and have no approved medical use. Nonetheless, experience in drug regulation under these treaties has given WHO and medicines regulatory agencies considerable expertise in identifying the characteristics of substance and drug formulations that influence dependence potential.

It has long been understood that the formulation and route of administration of a drug can influence its dependence potential (*27,33,69,70*). Perhaps the most dramatic example was crack cocaine, developed and marketed in the 1980s by illicit drug manufacturers and purveyors. Increasing abuse of prescription medicines in many countries since the 1990s has, however, stimulated research, expert conferences and the attention of medicines regulatory agencies on the importance of formulations in the dependence potential and attractiveness of drugs (e.g. *34*). Opioid analgesic formulations are of particular interest because factors such as the ease with which formulations can be manipulated so as to yield smokable and injectable products or crushed to produce more rapid effects by the oral route are major determinants of their attractiveness to drug abusers and their dependence potential (*69–71*). As these examples illustrate, dependence is not due simply to the dependence-producing drug but also to its route of delivery, dosage, formulation and many other factors that affect its pharmacological effects, and also behavioural factors, including product attractiveness. On the basis of such understanding, medicines regulatory authorities are requiring more restrictive risk management in the formulation of drugs with high dependence potential and attractiveness and finding ways to reduce restrictions on formulations that have less dependence potential.

Pharmaceutical regulation has led to half a century of experience in scientific evaluation of dependence potential. Guidance documents for research, the pharmaceutical industry and regulatory agencies have been updated every few years since the 1980s (e.g. *72*). Since 2003, the College on Problems of Drug Dependence has issued three updates (*37,39,73,74*). The WHO Expert Committee on Drug Dependence publishes annual evaluations and has issued reviews of methods less frequently (*42*). The most recent comprehensive guidance document on dependence potential is from the United States (*73*). Use of these methods to evaluate tobacco products showed that these products do meet the criteria for addictive drugs and that the dependence potential of nicotine varies widely, from minimally dependence-producing transdermal patches and nicotine chewing-gum to the most highly addictive route of nicotine delivery, cigarette smoke (*32,75*). In 2010, a conference of experts in dependence potential assessment and consumer product attractiveness issued a report to guide research, testing and regulation of tobacco products as a function of their dependence potential and attractiveness (*65*).

Dependence potential and product attractiveness and other factors that modulate tobacco product use, risk for dependence and harm

The risk for initiation, development of dependence and persistence of use of a tobacco product is related to both its dependence potential and attractiveness (*25,30,35,42,65*). These conclusions are based both on examination of tobacco industry documents, which revealed the efforts of the industry to design and manufacture products to increase their dependence potential and attractiveness, and WHO assessments, as discussed earlier. For a regulatory framework to reduce dependence potential, the evaluation should include an examination of the factors that influence attractiveness. Both tobacco industry documents and some non-industry research indicate that certain factors that increase dependence potential may also increase attractiveness and certain factors that increase attractiveness could increase the risk for dependence, even if they do not alter the pharmacological effects of the product. For example, there is no evidence that the manipulation or addition of acetaldehyde and ammonia compounds to cigarettes would increase their attractiveness, but these compounds could increase the pharmacological impact and dependence potential of cigarettes (*45,51,53*). Similarly, manipulation of pH to modify buffering chemicals in smokeless tobacco products is a key to manipulating the nicotine delivery of many such products, with the intent of developing and maintaining dependence, even though these substances are not known to be attractive to consumers (*25,76,77*).

Conversely, many factors in the design of tobacco products make them more attractive to targeted consumer populations and could increase the risk for dependence by encouraging use and repeated use. These include manipulating the sensory characteristics of tobacco products by the addition of colours and flavourings, packaging, marketing promotions and implicit claims of health effects (*30,56,67,68,78,79*). Menthol is clearly an important branding tool, which makes certain cigarette brands more attractive to many young people and targeted populations (e.g. African Americans in Canada and the United States); it may facilitate the development of dependence and increase smoke intake due to its throat-soothing effect. It is not clear, however, whether menthol directly increases the pharmacological impact of nicotine in the way that acetaldehyde and ammonia compounds appear to do (*79,80*). Many other substances added to tobacco products, such as laevulinic acid and urea, may contribute to smoke inhalation and dependence by making the smoke feel smoother and less irritating; chocolate may be added in such small amounts that the consumer does not characterize the smoke as 'chocolate' but finds the smoke more attractive (*52,79,81*). Physical design features may also contribute to dependence by making smoke easier to inhale and nicotine transfer to target receptors more efficient (e.g. by increasing the free base fraction of nicotine in the smoke), such as filter ventilation and smoke particle size (*35,51,53,54,82*).

In addition to product design and content, which modify dependence potential and attractiveness, marketing strategies such as advertising, price promotion, package size and access have been used by the tobacco industry to increase opportunities for initiation and dependence. Tobacco control strategies, including those embodied by the WHO FCTC, are increasingly designed to counteract these approaches and have been effective in reducing initiation and dependence and supporting cessation. The factors include increasing the cost (e.g. by increasing taxes on tobacco), decreasing access to and the number of places in which tobacco use is allowed (such as by banning sales to minors and enacting clean air laws), effective communication about harm, denormalizing and removing images of glamour and desirability, and providing treatment for dependent people.

Challenges in regulating tobacco products as compared with drug products

Evaluation of the dependence potential of pharmaceuticals is based on half a century of studies in experimental animals and humans, resulting in validated methods and also understanding of the limits of their generalizability (*37,73*). Most of the pharmaceuticals that have been evaluated for dependence potential have one active ingredient that is presumed to account for the most of the problems of abuse and dependence in the real world. Studies of how combinations of drugs increase or decrease dependence-producing and reinforcing effects have also been conducted with a variety of addictive drugs, including nicotine (*33,45,83–86*), and these methods could be used to examine the combinations of substances found in tobacco products more systematically (*75*). Furthermore, during the past decade, the importance of how a drug is formulated was increasingly recognized by regulatory agencies and pharmaceutical companies as a determinant of its attractiveness and dependence-producing effects.

Evaluating how the design of a complex pharmaceutical product can contribute to its attractiveness is more challenging than evaluating a relatively simple product that immediately releases its drug after oral, injected or other route of administration (*33*). Cigarettes and smokeless tobacco products are complex formulations, with physical design factors such as the size of the tobacco cutting, the size of smoke particles and diverse components that may have their own pharmacological effects or modulate the speed and impact of delivered nicotine (*25,62*). Furthermore, the emissions of smoked products contain many substances that are not present in unburnt tobacco products but are produced by pyrolysis (e.g. carbon monoxide and 'tar') and substances that are present in the unburnt product but are altered or increased in concentration in the smoke (e.g. acetaldehyde) (*25,62,75*).

The dependence potential of tobacco products has been studied for several decades, and the scientific basis for evaluating these products is increasing rapidly (*25,75*). Furthermore, recent reports have elucidated the diversity of the factors that contribute to tobacco product dependence potential and attractiveness, illustrating the challenges to their assessment (*30,53,75*). Although tobacco product dependence potential is generally more complex and more challenging to evaluate than that of pharmaceutical products, this need not delay the development of a regulatory framework. The science in this area is becoming stronger, and science-based regulation should proceed, with appropriate caution depending on the limits of the evidence.

The application of drug regulations differs from the proposed framework for reducing tobacco product dependence potential. In the case of pharmaceutical products, the regulations are used primarily to guide control in accordance with international treaties and national regulatory frameworks. The United States Controlled Substances Act drug scheduling provisions and similar frameworks in many other countries provide an incentive for pharmaceutical developers to design products with the lowest possible dependence potential, so as to meet the highly restrictive regulatory requirements and receive approval of their products for marketing (*36*). In the case of tobacco products, the regulatory framework is not proposed as a basis for approval or controlled substances scheduling but rather to guide regulators in setting standards for products and emissions (see also *25,62*). Countries are taking various approaches to such regulation. For example, Canada already bans many ingredients that are accepted in most other countries (*41*). The United

States, in accordance with the law establishing regulation of tobacco by its Food and Drug Administration, evaluates product contents for regulation on the basis of their potential to contribute to dependence and harm (*73,87*).

The law establishing Food and Drug Administration regulation of tobacco in the United States, the Family Smoking Prevention and Tobacco Control Act (Tobacco Control Act), has provisions to guide the evaluation of products with respect to dependence potential and to provide the basis for detecting the potential impact of the regulation, so that the approach can be modified if necessary. In setting performance standards and evaluating new and modified products, the Food and Drug Administration must consider:

- the risks and benefits to the population as a whole, covering users and nonusers of tobacco products;
- the increased or decreased likelihood that existing users of tobacco products will stop using such products; and
- the increased or decreased likelihood that those who do not use tobacco products will start using them.

The law requires that the effects be evaluated at population level by surveillance to ensure timely detection of public health consequences, intended and unintended, in order to avoid repeating the devastating problem posed by 'light' cigarettes, which persisted for several decades. Regulation therefore proceeds on the basis of the available scientific information, recognizing that the consequences, desired and undesired, might not be accurately predicted, but, if they are not, that they will be detected in a timely manner.

Nicotine policy

The main addictive substance that accounts for the dependence potential of tobacco products is nicotine. Therefore, it is vital that regulatory agencies establish guidance and standards for nicotine regulation, in order to prevent the development of dependence in new users and to achieve abstinence in current users by stopping the tobacco industry from including nicotine at levels that maintain or increase dependence potential. Nicotine is already regulated in pharmaceutical products for treating tobacco dependence and withdrawal. Although the content and delivered dosage of any pharmaceutical product is critical for product approval and acceptability for marketing, there are no such standards for nicotine in tobacco products. In the absence of standards and guidance, the nicotine levels in marketed products vary by more than 500 times (*25,77*). Tobacco companies have thus been free to set any nicotine level they choose to serve their end of increasing tobacco use and dependence, regardless of the harm to public health. Furthermore, tobacco companies have exploited the nicotine and 'tar' smoking machine test methods of the ISO and United States Federal Trade Commission to obtain nicotine and 'tar' ratings that mislead consumers, as they are much lower than those that can easily be obtained from smoking (*62,88,89*).

The level and speed of nicotine delivery from smokeless tobacco products, such as 'chewing tobacco', snuff and *snus*, is further controlled by the tobacco industry by use of pH-modifying buffers, which has resulted in products that vary widely in their dependence-producing effects (*76,90*). Thus, the industry makes and markets low-dose 'starter' products intended to initiate tobacco use and dependence and makes and markets very high-dose 'maintenance' products to maximize dependence and the difficulty of achieving abstinence (*25,77,90*). This is not acceptable.

There are no standards for tobacco product content, although some countries and the European Union have established upper limits on the amounts of 'tar' and nicotine that can be delivered, as measured by the ISO method. Insofar as this method is not recognized as valid by WHO (*88,91*) and its equivalent in the United States was rescinded by the Federal Trade Commission (*92*), this is not considered a valid approach for regulating nicotine.

The scientific basis for nicotine regulation has been evaluated by researchers participating in a series of meetings (*29*). Furthermore, methods exist to measure nicotine accurately in a wide range of tobacco products and emissions (*82,90*). It is therefore possible to regulate nicotine on the basis of its actual content and to provide consumers with information about nicotine content in measures such as the amount by weight in the product. Thus, there is a scientific foundation for developing policies to regulate nicotine content and emissions, so as to reduce or at least not enhance dependence potential.

The report of Hatsukami et al. (*29*) outlined a nicotine reduction strategy in which the nicotine content of cigarettes would eventually be reduced to levels that could not sustain pharmacological dependence, as discussed in earlier proposals (*93,94*). These reports discussed the limitations of the scientific understanding, the social acceptability and the preparedness of countries for such a strategy; they also identified areas in which research is needed. The research areas identified include determining the threshold dose of nicotine necessary to produce dependence, evaluating the effects of cigarettes with reduced nicotine on the brains of people who use them, examining potential public acceptance and evaluating unintended consequences. Henningfield et al. (*94*) described initiatives that would prepare countries for such a policy, including educating health professionals and tobacco users and ensuring that people who need treatment have access to it.

Regardless of whether a global nicotine policy reduces the amount to levels that do not produce dependence or allows a content that could sustain dependence but with reduced dependence potential and attractiveness, many of the scientific issues and research are the same. They include better understanding of the dose–response relation between nicotine administration and dependence and how various pharmacological and non-pharmacological factors alter dependence potential and the risk for dependence. This document does not recommend adoption of the approach of reducing nicotine to non-dependence-producing levels. The first step will be to exert regulatory control over nicotine content and communications, as discussed in this report and elsewhere (*25,59,95*). This will represent important progress towards a global nicotine policy.

Conclusions

- Tobacco products are designed and manufactured to increase their dependence potential.
- The dependence potential of tobacco products is due mainly to their delivery of nicotine.
- The dependence-producing effect of nicotine can be manipulated by designs that increase or decrease the amount and speed of nicotine delivery and absorption.
- The dependence potential of a product can be manipulated by designs that add ingredients with dependence-producing effects to the product and emissions, in addition to nicotine.
- Tobacco products have been extensively manipulated to make them attractive to target populations, to promote initiation and maintenance of tobacco use.
- Reducing the dependence potential and attractiveness of tobacco products would contribute to overall efforts to reduce tobacco use and disease.
- A regulatory framework to reduce dependence potential is vital to reducing tobacco use and disease.
- A regulatory framework to reduce dependence potential should include a framework for reducing product attractiveness.
- Although reliable scientific research on the dependence potential of drugs has been applied to tobacco products, they are more complex than most drug products, and it might be difficult to test the dependence potential of products such as those that are smoked and to address questions such as the contribution of ventilation and smoke particle size manipulation to dependence potential.
- Nicotine content and delivered doses in marketed products vary by more than 500 times, as the doses and delivery characteristics set by tobacco

manufacturers are not subject to guidance or standards (with the exception of limits on machine-delivered ratings according to the flawed and misleading ISO method).

- Nicotine content and the doses delivered by tobacco products are selected by the tobacco industry to increase dependence potential and persistent use, without consideration for public health goals.
- Unregulated nicotine manipulation by the tobacco industry can undermine tobacco control efforts to support prevention and foster cessation of tobacco use.
- The pharmacological dependence potential of tobacco products would probably be largely eliminated by reducing nicotine to trace or non-dependence-producing levels; however, scientific studies are needed before decisions are made about how to reduce tobacco product dependence potential most effectively.

Recommendations for regulatory policy

- A regulatory policy is needed to reduce tobacco product dependence potential, which should include a reduction in tobacco product attractiveness.
- Regulation of dependence potential should include guidance and standards for nicotine content and emissions.
- The standards and approaches should be specific for each product category. For example, smokeless tobacco products characterized as low-dose nicotine 'starter' products might be banned, insofar as their purpose is not to satisfy the needs of existing users but to draw new users (primarily young people) into long-term nicotine use and dependence.
- Regulatory standards for product design, contents (including nicotine), emissions and attractiveness should be guided by their predicted public health impact, in which the overall goal is to reduce tobacco use and attributable disease and death.
- Regulation to reduce dependence potential should be accompanied by population surveillance to identify the effects, desired and undesired, in a timely manner in order to allow any modifications to the regulation as appropriate to protect public health. New surveillance should be set up as required.
- Regulatory approaches should include mechanisms for modifying standards and approaches on the basis of the results of surveillance and epidemiological studies.
- Regulatory policy for tobacco products should be harmonized as appropriate with regulatory policy to reduce drug and alcohol dependence and

disease, recognizing differences in products, health effects and sociocultural factors.

- This advisory does not recommend specific approaches to be used by States Parties to the FCTC, because the most appropriate, most viable policy will vary by country as a function of the nature of their tobacco problem, resources and other factors. This advisory does, however, recommend that a nicotine policy be set on the basis of emerging knowledge and the predicted impact on public health.
- Laboratory methods to assess the impact of tobacco product contents and design features on dependence potential should be similar to those established as valid for evaluating drugs other than tobacco (*73,75*).
- WHO and national frameworks for regulating and controlling the dependence potential of drugs should be evaluated in order to understand their application and limitations from the perspectives of science, law and the potential to improve public health.

Recommendations for research to guide and evaluate regulatory actions and implementation to reduce tobacco product dependence potential

- Quantitative studies should be conducted to determine the content and emissions of dependence potential-enhancing substances (e.g. acetaldehyde, ammonia compounds, anabasine, nornicotine) and physical characteristics that could affect dependence potential, such as the fraction of unprotonated (free base) nicotine in products and their emissions, the pH of the contents and emissions, and the size and aerodynamics of smoke particles.
- In vitro studies might be conducted to better understand the mechanisms of action of dependence, e.g. with nicotine receptor subpopulations and other neuronal pathways.
- Studies of behavioural pharmacology in experimental animals could be used to study the reinforcing effects of target constituents singly or in combination with nicotine and other components.
- Clinical studies should be conducted as far as ethically possible to evaluate the overall dependence potential of various products, perhaps modified by the presence or absence of designs and components of concern.
- Studies should be conducted in a population of the effectiveness on dependence potential of various approaches to nicotine regulation (including nicotine reduction, placing upper limits on content and nicotine supplementation).

4. Overall recommendations

The WHO Study Group on Tobacco Product Regulation has launched a series of reports to provide a scientific foundation for tobacco product regulation. In line with Articles 9 and 10 of the WHO FCTC, these reports identify approaches for the regulation of tobacco products. Such products pose significant issues for public health and tobacco control policy.

The report of the sixth meeting deals with two important aspects of tobacco product regulation: the dependence potential of tobacco products, and health risks from exposure to toxic metals in smokeless tobacco products and from cigarette smoke. Of the topics discussed at the meeting, these issues were deemed by the experts to be the most critical for the issuance of recommendations for regulation.

Recommendations regarding toxic elements in tobacco and in cigarette smoke

Main recommendations

Toxic metals and metalloids constitute one of the least studied major carcinogenic chemical classes in smokeless tobacco products and tobacco smoke. The analysis of toxic metals in tobacco is of concern to health. This report summarizes the available evidence on the health risks from exposure to toxic metals in smokeless tobacco products and from cigarette smoke. Given the number of metals or metalloids found in tobacco, owing in part to the incorporation into the tobacco plant of the metallic elements in soil where tobacco is grown, this report is limited to a discussion of toxic or carcinogenic metals reported at significant concentrations. Thus, although there are other toxic metals in tobacco that warrant investigation, the metals described in this report are considered of greatest concern due to their concentrations in tobacco or smoke, their carcinogenicity and other toxic effects. In this regard, a number of research recommendations are presented.

Significance for public health policies

The extent to which consumption of a particular tobacco product confers additional risks for exposure to toxic metals is an important question.

Smokeless tobacco products are consumed in different ways from cigarette tobacco or other tobacco products that are smoked. Whether the product is consumed in a smokeless form or by smoking influences overall exposure and the subsequent associated health risks directly to the tobacco consumer and possibly to people in close proximity who are exposed in the form of second-hand smoke. For example, some of the metals found in tobacco and tobacco smoke are known carcinogens. There is also strong biochemical and pathological evidence for airway sensitization and inflammation, including atopic inflammation, as a consequence of exposure to tobacco smoke particulate. Studies have also demonstrated that metals present in the particulate matter induce the production and release of inflammatory mediators by the respiratory tract. Similarly, oral exposure to individual metals may have an impact on health.

Implications for the Organization's programmes

There are five major classes of carcinogens in tobacco smoke, of which some have been carefully studied, contributing to a strong weight of evidence for associated health risks. Exposure to toxic metals from smokeless tobacco products and the associated health risks have been studied much less than inhalation of particulate metals. It is recognized that toxic metals and metalloids constitute one of the least studied major carcinogenic chemical classes in smokeless tobacco products and tobacco smoke. Thus, in order to provide better policy guidance to Member States in relation to smokeless tobacco products, the report recommends further studies on metal concentrations in smokeless tobacco, smokeless tobacco additives, and cigarette and waterpipe tobacco produced in all geographical areas. In addition, research should be conducted to determine the factors, including soil levels and environmental conditions, that lead to higher constituent levels of metals in tobacco products. Recommendations should be made to restrict the growth of tobacco in regions with a high soil metal content. Given that the consumption of a particular tobacco product confers additional risks for exposure to toxic metals, WHO should recommend a broader research agenda, including the study of metals or metalloids that are, according to the classifications of the International Agency for Research on Cancer, group 1 human carcinogens, group 2A probable human carcinogens, or group 2B possible human carcinogens.

Recommendations on the basis for a regulatory framework to reduce the dependence potential of tobacco products

Main recommendations

The foundation for a regulatory framework to reduce tobacco-product dependence potential is scientific understanding of the determinants of tobacco dependence and evidence that the design and manufacture of tobacco products can increase or decrease dependence potential. The primary dependence-producing constituent of tobacco is nicotine. Tobacco products are designed to optimize the addictive effects of nicotine, whereas nicotine replacement therapy products are designed to minimize them. Several decades of research have shown that the dependence-producing effects of nicotine are directly influenced by the dose and speed of nicotine absorption, by other ingredients and design features, and by associated sensory and environmental stimuli. Tobacco companies have understood this for many decades and used this knowledge to optimize dosing characteristics and employ ingredients and designs to optimize dependence potential. Designs and ingredients were also intended to increase product attractiveness to and ease of initiation of young people, women and other target populations. This recommendation has been prepared because tobacco companies have not been restricted in their ability to design and manufacture products to increase dependence potential and attractiveness; the intent of the companies is to increase tobacco product use and dependence by undermining prevention and cessation tobacco control measures. This recommendation provides specific conclusions and recommendations for regulatory policies addressing a framework for reducing the dependence potential of tobacco products.

Significance for public health policies

Experience with pharmaceutical nicotine delivery systems and other drug delivery systems has demonstrated that dependence potential can be altered by the design of the product. For drug products, including smoking cessation medications, minimizing dependence potential is an explicit goal of manufacturers and regulators. Although tobacco products are exempt from such international and national drug regulatory controls and frameworks, such regulatory approaches demonstrate that dependence potential and attractiveness can be regulated. The principles and experience applied to drug regulation could be applied to tobacco product regulation in order to ensure that they are no longer designed and manufactured to optimize dependence potential and attractiveness. The WHO Study Group on Tobacco Product Regulation maintains that a regulatory framework to reduce the dependence potential and attractiveness of tobacco products could improve public health by contributing to more effective tobacco control to reduce initiation, the prevalence of tobacco use and resulting morbidity and mortality.

Implications for the Organization's programmes

In the light of strategies employed by the tobacco industry to manipulate the nicotine-dosing capacity of its products and, consequently, increase tobacco-product dependence potential, WHO should promote approaches that could be used to reduce dependence potential under a regulatory framework. In so far as the main addictive substance in tobacco is nicotine, WHO should provide guidance to Member States concerning the scientific foundation and potential approaches for a regulatory framework to reduce the dependence potential of tobacco products. This should be undertaken with the aim of reducing the prevalence of tobacco use and harm by reducing the risk and severity of dependence as a biological force that contributes to the perpetuation of tobacco use. As tobacco products pose certain challenges that are more complex and may be more difficult to address than those posed by regulated drug products, WHO should support better understanding of the dose–response relation between nicotine administration and dependence and how various pharmacological and non-pharmacological factors alter dependence potential and the risk for dependence.

5. References

1. International Agency for Research on Cancer. *Overall evaluations of carcinogenicity to humans*. Lyon, 2011. http://monographs.iarc.fr/ENG/Classification/index.php (accessed 1 November 2011).
2. Pappas RS et al. Analysis of toxic metals in commercial moist snuff and Alaska iqmik. *Journal of Analytical Toxicology*, 2008, 32:281–291.
3. Rickert WS et al. Chemical and toxicological characterization of commercial smokeless tobacco products available on the Canadian market. *Regulatory Toxicology and Pharmacology*, 2009, 53:121–133.
4. Shaikh AN et al. Determination of some toxic trace elements in Indian tobacco and its smoke. *Journal of Radioanalytical and Nuclear Chemistry*, 1992, 163:349–353.
5. Dhaware D et al. Determination of toxic metals in Indian smokeless tobacco products. *Scientific World Journal*, 2009, 9:1140–1147.
6. Addo MA et al. Mineral profile of Ghanaian dried tobacco leaves and local snuff: a comparative study. *Journal of Radioanalytical and Nuclear Chemistry*, 2008, 277:517–524.
7. Hammond D, O'Connor RJ. Constituents in tobacco and smoke emissions from Canadian cigarettes. *Tobacco Control*, 2008, 17:i24–i31.
8. Kazi TG et al. Determination of toxic elements in different brands of cigarette by atomic absorption spectrometry using ultrasonic assisted acid digestion. *Environmental Monitoring and Assessment*, 2009, 154:155–167.
9. Swami K, Judd CD, Orsini J. Trace metals analysis of legal and counterfeit cigarette tobacco samples using inductively coupled plasma mass spectrometry and cold vapor atomic absorption spectrometry. *Spectroscopy Letters*, 2009, 42:479–490.
10. Stephens WE, Calder A, Newton J. Source and health implications of high toxic metal concentrations in illicit tobacco products. *Environmental Science and Technology*, 2005, 39:479–488.
11. Counts ME et al. Smoke composition and predicting relationships for international commercial cigarettes smoked with three machine-smoking conditions. *Regulatory Toxicology Pharmacology*, 2005, 41:185–227.
12. Hoffmann D et al. Toxic and carcinogenic agents in moist and dry snuff. *Journal of the National Cancer Institute*, 1987, 79:1281–1286.

13. Verma S, Yadav S, Singh I. Trace metal concentration in different Indian tobacco products and related health implications. *Food and Chemical Toxicology*, 2010, 48:2291–2297.

14. Pappas RS et al. Cadmium, lead, and thallium in mainstream tobacco smoke particulate. *Food and Chemical Toxicology*, 2006, 44:714–723.

15. Syed U-F, Bari A, Husain L. Leaching of 210Po in human saliva from smokeless tobacco. *Journal of Radioanalytical and Nuclear Chemistry*, 2009, 281:541–546.

16. Peres AC, Hiromoto G. Evaluation of 210Pb and 210Po from cigarette tobacco produced in Brazil. *Journal of Environmental Radioactivity*, 2002, 62:115–119.

17. Papastefanou C. Radiation dose from cigarette tobacco. *Radiation Protection Dosimetry*, 2007, 123:68–73.

18. Savidou A, Kehagia K, Eleftheriadis K. Concentration levels of 210Pb and 210Po in dry tobacco leaves in Greece. *Journal of Environmental Radioactivity*, 2006, 85:94–102.

19. Desideri D et al. 210Po and 210Pb inhalation by cigarette smoking in Italy. *Health Physics*, 2007, 92:58–63.

20. Schayer S et al. ^{210}Po and ^{210}Pb activity in Chinese cigarettes. *Health Physics*, 2009, 96:543–549.

21. Food and Drug Administration. Regulations restricting the sale and distribution of cigarettes and smokeless tobacco to protect children and adolescents; final rule. *Federal Register*, 1996, 61:44396–45318.

22. Royal College of Physicians. *Nicotine addiction in Britain, a report of the Tobacco Advisory Group of the Royal College of Physicians*, London, 2000.

23. National Cancer Institute. *The role of the media in promoting and reducing tobacco use*. Bethesda, Maryland, United States Department of Health and Human Services, National Institutes of Health, 2008 (Tobacco Control Monograph No. 19; NIH Pub. No. 07-6242).

24. World Health Organization. *Advancing knowledge on regulating tobacco products*. Geneva, 2001.

25. World Health Organization. *The scientific bases of tobacco product regulation; report of a WHO study group (TobReg)*. Geneva, 2007 (WHO Technical Report Series, No. 945).

26. United States Department of Health and Human Services. *The health consequences of smoking—nicotine addiction: a report of the Surgeon General,* Washington DC, Government Printing Office, 1988.

27. College on Problems of Drug Dependence. *Policy on nicotine and tobacco*. Philadelphia, Pennsylvania, 1995. Available at http://www.cpdd.vcu.edu/Pages/FactSheets/Tobacco.html (accessed 4 December 2010).

28. Henningfield JE, Benowitz NL. Pharmacology of tobacco addiction. In: Boyle P et al., eds. *Tobacco and public health: science and policy*, 2nd ed. Oxford, Oxford University Press, 2010:155–170.

29. Hatsukami DK et al. Nicotine reduction revisited: science and future directions. *Tobacco Control*, 2010, 19:e1–e10 (doi:10.1136/tc.2009).

30. Scientific Committee on Emerging and Newly Identified Health Risks. *Addictiveness and attractiveness of tobacco additives*. Brussels, European Commission, 2010.

31. United States Surgeon General. *The health consequences of smoking: how tobacco causes disease. A report of the Surgeon General*. Washington DC, United States Public Health Service, Centers for Disease Control, Center for Health Promotion and Education, Office on Smoking and Health, United States Department of Health and Human Services, 2010.

32. Stitzer ML, DeWitt H. Abuse liability of nicotine. In: Benowitz NL, ed. *Nicotine safety and toxicity*. New York, Oxford University Press, 1998: 119–131.

33. Grudzinskas C et al. Impact of formulation on the abuse liability, safety, and regulation of medications: the expert panel report. *Drug and Alcohol Dependence*, 2006, 83(Suppl.):S77–S82.

34. Sellers EM, Schuster CR. Conference on drug formulations and abuse liability. *Drug and Alcohol Dependence*, 2006, 83(Suppl.):S1–S3.

35. Wayne GF, Carpenter CM. Manipulating product design to reinforce tobacco addiction. In: Boyle P et al., eds. *Tobacco: science, policy, and public health*. Oxford, Oxford University Press, 2010:171–195.

36. Spillane J, McAllister WB. Keeping the lid on: a century of drug regulation and control. *Drug and Alcohol Dependence*, 2003, 70(Suppl):S5–S12.

37. Expert Panel. Abuse liability assessment of CNS drugs: conclusions, recommendations, and research priorities. *Drug and Alcohol Dependence*, 2003, 70(Suppl):S107–S114.

38. Henningfield JE, Schuster CR. Risk management and post-marketing surveillance of CNS drugs: commentary. *Drug and Alcohol Dependence*, 2009, 105(Suppl):S56–S64.

39. Johanson C-E et al. Risk management and post-marketing surveillance for the abuse of medications acting on the central nervous system: Expert Panel report. *Drug and Alcohol Dependence*, 2009, 105(Suppl): S65–S71.

40. European Medicines Agency. *Questions and answers on the review of modified-release oral opioid medicines of the WHO level III scale for the management of pain. Outcome of a procedure under Article 31 of Directive 2001/83/EC as amended*. London, 2010. Available at: http://www.ema.europa.eu/docs/en_GB/document_library/Referrals_document/Modified-released_oral_opioids_31/WC500099180.pdf (accessed 4 December 2010).

41. Health Canada. *Opioid pain medications: frequently asked questions*. Ottawa, 2010. Available at: http://www.hc-sc.gc.ca/hl-vs/iyh-vsv/med/opioid-faq-opioides-eng.php#a14 (accessed 4 December 2010).
42. World Health Organization Expert Committee on Drug Dependence. *Management of substance abuse*. Geneva, 2010. Available at http://www.who.int/substance_abuse/right_committee/en/index.html (accessed 23 November 2010).
43. Slade J et al. Nicotine and addiction: the Brown and Williamson documents. *Journal of the American Medical Association*, 1995, 274: 225–233.
44. *United States of America v. Philip Morris USA Inc., et al.*, Civil Action No. 99-cv-02496 (GK). Written direct testimony of Victor J. Denoble, II, PhD. Available at http://www.justice.gov/civil/cases/tobacco2/DeNoble_USwritten%20direct.pdf (accessed 29 December 2011).
45. DeNoble VJ, Mele PC. Intravenous nicotine self-administration in rats: effects of mecamylamine, hexamethonium and naloxone. *Psychopharmacology*, 2006, 184:266-272.
46. Barry H. Censorship by a tobacco company. *Psychopharmacology*, 2006, 184:273.
47. Food and Drug Administration. 21 CFR Part 801. Regulations restricting the sale and distribution of cigarettes and smokeless tobacco products to protect children and adolescents; proposed rule analysis regarding FDA's jurisdiction over nicotine-containing cigarettes and smokeless tobacco products; notice. *Federal Register*, 1995, 60:41314–41792.
48. Food and Drug Administration. 21 CFR Part 801. Regulations restricting the sale and distribution of cigarettes and smokeless tobacco to protect children and adolescents; final rule. *Federal Register*, 61:44396–45318 (1996).
49. Davis RM, Douglas CE, Beasley JK. The Tobacco Deposition and Trial Testimony Archive (DATTA) project: origins, aims, and methods. *Tobacco Control*, 2006, 15(Suppl IV): iv4–iv8.
50. Hurt RD, Robertson CR. Prying open the door to the tobacco industry's secrets about nicotine: the Minnesota Tobacco Trial. *Journal of the American Medical Association*, 1998, 280:1173–1181.
51. Wayne GF, Connolly GN, Henningfield JE. Assessing internal tobacco industry knowledge of the neurobiology of tobacco dependence. *Nicotine and Tobacco Research*, 2004, 6:927–940.
52. Megerdichian CL et al. Internal tobacco industry research on olfactory and trigeminal nerve response to nicotine and other smoke components. *Nicotine and Tobacco Research*, 2007, 9:1119–1129.
53. Wayne GF, Connolly GN, Henningfield JE. Brand differences of free-base nicotine delivery in cigarette smoke: the view of the tobacco industry documents. *Tobacco Control*, 2006, 15:189–198.

54. Wayne FE et al. Tobacco industry research and efforts to manipulate smoke particle size: implications for product regulation. *Nicotine and Tobacco Research*, 2008, 10:613–625.

55. Wayne GF, Henningfield JE. *Tobacco product attractiveness as a contributor to tobacco addiction and disease. Report to Health Canada by commission.* Ottawa, Health Canada, 2008.

56. National Cancer Institute. *Monograph 19: The role of the media in promoting and reducing tobacco use.* Washington DC, Department of Health and Human Services, National Institutes of Health, National Cancer Institute, 2008 (NIH Pub. No. 07-6242).

57. World Health Organization. *Draft guidelines for the implementation of Articles 9 and 10 of the World Health Organization Framework Convention on Tobacco Control.* Framework Convention on Tobacco Control Conference of the Parties, 2010. Fourth session, Punta del Este, Uruguay, November 2010, agenda item 5.2, page 5. Geneva, 2010. Available at http://apps.who.int/gb/fctc/PDF/cop4/FCTC_COP4_6Rev1-en.pdf. (accessed 29 November 2010).

58. Government of Canada. *An act to amend the Tobacco Act, assented to 8 October 2009.* Ottawa. Available at http://www.parl.gc.ca/content/hoc/Bills/402/Government/C-32/C-32_4/C-32_4.pdf (accessed 29 December 2011).

59. World Health Organization. *Scientific Advisory Committee on Tobacco Product Regulation. Recommendation on nicotine and the regulation of tobacco and non-tobacco products.* Geneva, 2003.

60. World Health Organization. *Scientific Advisory Committee on Tobacco Product Regulation. Recommendation on tobacco product ingredients and emissions.* Geneva, 2003.

61. World Health Organization. *Scientific Advisory Committee on Tobacco Product Regulation. Statement of principles guiding the evaluation of new or modified tobacco products.* Geneva, 2003.

62. World Health Organization. *Study Group on Tobacco Product Regulation. Recommendation: guiding principles for the development of tobacco product research and testing capacity and proposed protocols for the initiation of tobacco product testing.* Geneva, 2004.

63. World Health Organization. *The scientific basis of tobacco product regulation; report of a WHO study group (TobReg).* Geneva, 2009 (WHO Technical Report Series, No. 955).

64. Schuster CR, Henningfield JE. Conference on abuse liability assessment of CNS drugs: introduction. *Drug and Alcohol Dependence*, 2003, 70:S1–S4.

65. Henningfield JE et al. Conference on abuse liability and appeal of tobacco products: conclusions and recommendations. *Drug and Alcohol Dependence*, 2011, 116:1–7.

66. Pierce JP et al. Camel no. 9 cigarette-marketing campaign targeted young teenage girls. *Pediatrics*, 2010, 125:619–626.

67. Rees VW et al. Assessing consumer responses to potential reduced-exposure tobacco products: a review of tobacco industry and independent research methods. *Cancer Epidemiology, Biomarkers and Prevention*, 2009, 12:3225–3240.

68. Slovic P. *Smoking: risk, perception and policy.* Thousand Oaks, California, Sage Publishers, 2001.

69. Sellers EM, Schuster CR. Conference on drug formulations and abuse liability. *Drug and Alcohol Dependence*, 2006, 83(Suppl 1):S1–S3.

70. O'Brien CP. Drug addiction and drug abuse. In: Brunton LL, Lazo JS, Parker KL. *Goodman and Gilman's The Pharmacological Basis of Therapeutics*, 11th ed, New York, McGraw-Hill, 2006:607–627.

71. National Institute on Drug Abuse. *Drugs, brains, and behavior: the science of addiction.* Bethesda, Maryland: National Institutes of Health, 2010. Available at http://www.drugabuse.gov/scienceofaddiction/sciofaddiction.pdf (accessed 29 December 2011).

72. Balster RL, Bigelow GE. Guidelines and methodological reviews concerning drug abuse liability assessment. *Drug and Alcohol Dependence*, 2003, 70(Suppl. 3):S13–S40.

73. Food and Drug Administration. *Draft guidance for industry: assessment of abuse potential of drugs.* Washington DC, 2010. Available at http://www.fda.gov/downloads/Drugs/GuidanceComplianceRegulatoryInformation/Guidances/UCM198650.pdf (accessed 29 December 2011).

74. Carter LP, Griffiths RR. Principles of laboratory assessment of drug abuse liability and implications for clinical development. *Drug and Alcohol Dependence*, 2009, 105(Suppl. 1):S14–S25.

75. Carter LP et al. Abuse liability assessment of tobacco products including potential reduced exposure products. *Cancer Epidemiology, Biomarkers and Prevention*, 2009, 18:3241–3262.

76. Fant RV et al. Pharmacokinetics and pharmacodynamics of moist snuff in humans. *Tobacco Control*, 1999, 8:387–392.

77. Scientific Committee on Emerging and Newly Identified Health Risks. *Scientific opinion on the health effects of smokeless tobacco products.* Brussels, European Commission, 2008.

78. Ling PM, Glantz SA. Why and how the tobacco industry sell cigarettes to young adults: evidence from industry documents. *American Journal of Public Health*, 2002, 92:908–916.

79. Wayne GF, Carpenter CM. Manipulating product design to reinforce tobacco addiction. In: Boyle P et al., eds. *Tobacco and public health: science and policy*, 2nd ed. Oxford, Oxford University Press, 2010: 171–195.

80. Tobacco Products Scientific Advisory Committee. *Menthol cigarettes and public health: review of the scientific evidence and recommendations.* Washington DC, Food and Drug Administration, 2010. Available at http://www.fda.gov/downloads/AdvisoryCommittees/CommitteesMeetingMaterials/TobaccoProductsScientificAdvisoryCommittee/UCM247689.pdf (accessed 29 December 2011).

81. Henningfield JE et al. Reducing tobacco addiction through tobacco product regulation. *Tobacco Control*, 2004, 13:132–135.

82. Ashley DL et al. Approaches, challenges, and experience in assessing free nicotine. In: Henningfield JE, London ED, Pogun S, eds. *Nicotine psychopharmacology*. Berlin, Springer-Verlag, 2006:437–456 (Handbook of Experimental Pharmacology, No. 192).

83. Goldberg SR, Spealman RD, Goldberg DM. Persistent behavior at high rates maintained by intravenous self -administration of nicotine. *Science*, 1981, 214:573–575.

84. Goldberg SR et al. Control of behavior by intravenous nicotine injections in laboratory animals. *Pharmacology, Biochemistry and Behavior*, 1983, 19:1011–1020.

85. Le Foll B, Goldberg SR. Effects of nicotine in experimental animals and humans: an update on addictive properties. In: Henningfield JE, London ED, Pogun S, eds. *Nicotine psychopharmacology*. Berlin, Springer-Verlag, 2006:335–368 (Handbook of Experimental Pharmacology, No. 192).

86. Winger G et al. Relative reinforcing effects of cocaine, remifentanil, and their combination in rhesus monkeys. *Journal of Pharmacology and Experimental Therapeutics*, 2006, 318:223–229.

87. United States Congress. *Family smoking prevention and tobacco control act. Public law # 111-31*. Washington DC, 2009. Available at http://frwebgate.access.gpo.gov/cgi-bin/getdoc.cgi?dbname=111_cong_public_laws&docid=f:publ031.111.pdf. (accessed 25 June 2010).

88. World Health Organization. *Recommendation on health claims derived from ISO/FTC method to measure cigarette yield.* Geneva, 2002.

89. National Cancer Institute. *Risks associated with smoking cigarettes with low machine-measured yields*. Bethesda, Maryland, National Institutes of Health, 2001 (Smoking and Tobacco Control Monograph 13).

90. Djordjevic MV, Doran KA. Nicotine content and delivery across tobacco products. In: Henningfield JE, London ED, Pogun S, eds. *Nicotine psychopharmacology*. Berlin, Springer-Verlag, 2006:61–82 (Handbook of Experimental Pharmacology, No. 192).

91. World Health Organization. *Best practices in tobacco control. Regulation of tobacco products. Canada report.* Geneva, 2005. Available at http://www.who.int/tobacco/publications/prod_regulation/canadian_best_practices/en/index.html.

92. Federal Trade Commission. *FTC rescinds guidance from 1966 on statements concerning tar and nicotine yields*. Washington DC, 2008. Available at http://www.ftc.gov/opa/2008/11/cigarettetesting.shtm (accessed 29 December 2011).

93. Benowitz NL, Henningfield JE. Establishing a nicotine threshold for addiction. *New England Journal of Medicine*, 1994, 331:123–125.

94. Henningfield JE et al. Reducing the addictiveness of cigarettes. *Tobacco Control*, 1998, 7:281–293.

95. Hatsukami DK et al. Nicotine reduction revisited: science and future directions. *Tobacco Control*, 2010, 19:e1–e10 (doi:10.1136/tc.2009).

Annex 1

Toxic elements in tobacco and in cigarette smoke

R.S. Pappas, PhD, Team Lead, Tobacco Inorganic Group, Emergency Response and Air Toxicants Branch, Centers for Disease Control and Prevention, Atlanta, Georgia, United States of America

Preface

The extent to which consumption of a particular tobacco product poses additional risks for exposure to toxic metals is an important question. Many factors must be considered, such as the form of the product, where and under what conditions the tobacco in the product was cultivated, the manufacturing processes and treatments it underwent before marketing, the way the product is consumed and individual differences in consumption habits. Smokeless tobacco products are consumed differently from cigarettes and other smoking products, and the way in which a tobacco product is consumed determines the type of exposure and associated health risks for both the consumer and perhaps people in close proximity, such as by inhalation of second-hand smoke. This report summarizes the evidence on certain health risks associated with exposure to toxic metals in smokeless tobacco products and cigarette smoke.

Background

Nicotine is the most commonly known addictive, neuroteratogenic, toxic substance biologically available from tobacco, regardless of the manner in which the tobacco is consumed. Nicotine is, however, only one of many substances of concern in tobacco. Tobacco smoke contains five major classes of carcinogen (*1*), some of which have been carefully studied, providing a strong weight of evidence for the associated health risks (*2*). Tobacco-specific nitrosamines, for example, are a well-known group of toxic and carcinogenic substances that are biologically available from tobacco. Although present in all tobacco products, tobacco-specific nitrosamines have been found in especially high concentrations in certain smokeless products (*3*,*4*). Other constituents that are biologically available from all tobacco products are metals and metalloid ions.

Toxic metals and metalloids in smokeless tobacco products and tobacco smoke have not been widely studied. Eight of the 40 substances in Fowles and Dybing's (*1*) table of cancer risk indices are metals or metalloids, although silicates were not included. In their summary table of non-cancer risk chemical constituents of mainstream cigarette smoke, based on a smoking rate of a single cigarette per day, three of the eight substances with respiratory effects, cadmium, hexavalent chromium and nickel, are metals. One of the seven substances that pose a cardiovascular risk is arsenic, a metalloid.

Metals and metalloids in tobacco are generally present in ionic form and can therefore be present as positively charged ions or polyatomic species with a positive or a negative electrical charge. Metals and metalloids in smoke from biomass combustion, including tobacco, are generally considered to be present in ionic form as oxides, chlorides, carbonates, silicates or organic complexes, but may also occur in gaseous elemental form, as is the case for mercury (*5*) and gaseous complexes such as nickel and iron carbonyls, or possibly in elemental metallic form in aerosol particulate. Toxic metals and metalloids are often loosely called 'heavy metals', regardless of their atomic or molecular mass.

Some ions, such as sodium, potassium, magnesium, calcium, selenite, iodide, molybdenum, cobalt, copper, chromium in its +3 oxidation state (chromium [III]), manganese in its +2 oxidation state, nickel, zinc and others in trace amounts are considered to be nutrients and are necessary for cell and organ function in the body. At higher concentrations, however, many of the ions considered essential nutrients are toxic, carcinogenic or both. Other ions, such as aluminium, antimony, arsenic, barium, beryllium, bismuth, cadmium, chromium in its +6 oxidation state (chromium [VI]), lead, manganese in high oxidation states, mercury, nickel, polonium and thallium, are not known to be beneficial and are toxic (chemically or radioactively), carcinogenic or both.

The risks presented by metals in their elemental form has been incompletely evaluated. For example, inhaled metallic mercury rapidly enters the bloodstream; unoxidized mercury is hydrophobic and can cross membranes, including the blood–brain barrier. Elemental mercury is only partially oxidized to mercury [II] in the lungs and erythrocytes and, after clearance from the blood, may be oxidized by the brain and liver (*6*). Metallic forms of other metals may occur in smoke particulate, but no studies of other metallic forms were found in peer-reviewed literature.

Scope

Whether a tobacco product is consumed by smoking or in a smokeless form, exposure to toxic metals is directly related to the concentration in the tobacco leaf, assuming no metal-containing additives are added during manufacture (*7–9*). It is beyond the scope of this annex to discuss every metal and metalloid found in tobacco, because every metallic element in the soil in which tobacco is grown is likely be incorporated into the plants. It is more important to consider metals or metalloids that have been classified by working groups convened by the International Agency for Research on Cancer (IARC) in group 1, human carcinogens (such as arsenic, cadmium and nickel), group 2A, probable human carcinogens (such as lead), or group 2B, possible human carcinogens (such as cobalt), than more benign metals, such as calcium, magnesium, strontium, potassium and sodium. The discussion is therefore limited to toxic or carcinogenic metals reported to occur at significant concentrations in tobacco products or their emissions.

Although metal ions can be deposited on tobacco leaves from airborne particulate fall-out, and some toxic metal-containing fungicides and pesticides were, in the past, sprayed on tobacco leaves or soils (*10*), most of the metal content of tobacco plants is absorbed directly from the soil (*11–15*). Soil and any amendments to soil, such as sludge (which acidifies the soil), fertilizers and irrigation with polluted water are the predominant sources of the characteristic metal content of tobacco, which varies by geographical area (*16–22*). Therefore, high metal concentrations in soil or its amendments will result in high concentrations in tobacco crops grown on the soil.

For example, in 1980, almost 80% of cropland soil in China was deficient in phosphate, containing less than 10 mg/kg of soil. Over the past 30 years, the Government has put in place policies to encourage the use of phosphate fertilizers, and, as a result, the average phosphate content of the soil has nearly tripled (*23*). While this has increased crop production, phosphate, an excellent chelator of many metal ions, adds metals to the soil. Fertilization with animal waste, which acidifies the soil and has high concentrations of excreted toxic metals, increases the availability of metals from the soil. Together, these two practices have increased the levels of phosphate and metals in runoff wastewater, which is sometimes used for irrigation. As would be anticipated, the arsenic, cadmium and lead concentrations in Chinese cigarette tobacco are two to three times higher than those in Canadian cigarettes (*9*).

Instrumentation commonly used to analyse tobacco and smoke

Analytical methods for tobacco, except for neutron activation, generally require some sample preparation before quantification. The preparation often involves microwave digestion under pressure with nitric acid and other reagents, usually in a medium-to-high pressure system. The analysis of smoke requires the generation and collection of tobacco smoke samples. Mainstream smoke is usually divided into the gas phase and the particulate phase, although whole smoke is sometimes trapped. The concentrations of metals and other constituents in tobacco smoke generated by standardized smoking machines depend on the smoking regimen, which is defined by puff volume, puff frequency, puff duration and physical design parameters, including tobacco weight, paper porosity, filter efficiency and filter ventilation. The particulate phase is trapped on glass or, preferably, quartz fibre filters or by electrostatic precipitation. A smoking machine for the analysis of tobacco smoke should have enough flexibility to operate under standard machine smoking regimens, such as those specified by ISO or intense regimens such as that used by Health Canada.

Previously, tobacco and smoke were generally analysed by flame or graphite furnace atomic absorption spectrophotometry. The advantages of this instrumentation, especially graphite furnace atomic absorption, are low equipment cost and reliability; the disadvantages include less sensitivity than more recent instrumentation and lack of multi-element capability, so that the same sample must be analysed several times for different metals, which may lower throughput. The advantages of neutron activation analysis over atomic absorption are greater sensitivity and multi-element capability; however, a high-energy neutron source, such as a reactor, or highly regulated radionuclides are required, in addition to operator expertise, prohibiting its use for most analysts. Furthermore, the sample becomes highly radioactive and requires proper disposal. Inductively coupled plasma–mass spectrometry is currently the preferred instrumentation for laboratories that have sufficient funding and facilities, high-purity liquefied gas resources and the necessary expertise. It has multi-element capability and allows higher throughput than the other instrumentation described.

Toxic metals in smokeless tobacco products

Smokeless tobacco was evaluated by an IARC working group as a group 1 carcinogen, which is to say, carcinogenic to humans beyond a reasonable doubt (*24*). The pathological risks to which a consumer is exposed by consumption of smokeless tobacco arise from cumulative exposure to all the toxic, irritant and carcinogenic substances that are biologically available from the products; however, as toxicity and carcinogenesis are complex processes, different substances are usually studied individually. This annex focuses on the consequences of exposure to metals and metalloids in tobacco products.

Toxic metal concentrations in smoking tobacco have been reported more frequently than those in smokeless tobacco, and exposure to toxic metals from consumption of smokeless tobacco and the potential associated health risks have been studied even less. The epithelial tissues of the oral cavity have high proximal transfer potential, which permits absorption and transfer of toxic metals from smokeless tobacco products across the epithelial tissue, as illustrated for cadmium below. The oesophagus and stomach are exposed to metals dissolved in saliva and swallowed; systemic exposure probably occurs from direct oral absorption or absorption of swallowed saliva or tobacco particulate in the digestive tract. Exposure depends on the total concentration of a toxic metal in tobacco, direct transfer by contact with the oral mucosa, the transfer rates from the products and their solubility in saliva and digestive fluids. Therefore, estimates of exposure based on mean concentration in tobacco, extract or saliva may not represent the actual oral or body burden.

A few authors have reported the concentrations of extractable toxic metals in artificial or human saliva exposed to smokeless tobacco. The results of studies of metal extraction from artificial saliva indicate that metals are toxicants and carcinogens that are biologically available in the oral cavity. The artificial saliva used for extracting toxic metals from tobacco has included 0.1 mol/l phosphate buffer and several strong chelating agents (*25*) or saturated calcium phosphate, inorganic salts, sugars, enzymes and mucin (*26*). Rickert et al. (*27*) cited a formulation used by van Ruth et al. (*28*) but did not specify which of three artificial saliva model formulations (distilled water; inorganic salts in water; and inorganic salts, mucin and α-amylase) described by van Ruth et al., which were designed for extraction in various toxicity assays, rather than for quantitative analysis.

There is no standardized saliva formulation for tobacco extraction. The more closely the formula resembles average human saliva, the more meaningful the results in biological terms. Given sufficient extraction time, strong chelating agents like ethylenediaminetetraacetic acid (EDTA) or diethylene triamine pentaacetic acid (DTPA) can be used to extract many toxic metals in tobacco almost quantitatively into solution, but little is known about their extraction efficiency from human saliva. Water alone does not adequately reflect saliva; the addition of salts more closely imitates saliva, but, if phosphate is added without proteins and mucin, some metals may be undetected, as several of them co-precipitate as insoluble phosphates when tobacco is centrifuged or filtered from solution. As the mucin and protein functional groups can chelate metals, a formulation including these elements is more representative. Nevertheless, although a formulation containing appropriate salts, saturated or supersaturated calcium phosphate, proteins and mucin better represents saliva (*26*), the difficulty of preparing saturated or supersaturated calcium phosphate and the time required each day make it an impractical component of frequent analyses. A useful compromise formulation might contain calcium and phosphate at 25% or more below saturation to permit refrigeration without precipitation.

Toxic metals in smoked tobacco products

Inhaled mainstream cigarette smoke transports many substances through the mouth and throat and into the lungs, where a substantial portion of the particulate matter and volatiles are absorbed or deposited internally. Many of these substances are rapidly absorbed through the lungs, transferred efficiently to the bloodstream and distributed quickly through the circulatory system. Other smoke constituents, including 60–80% of particulate (*29*), are retained, accumulate in the lungs and gradually partition between the lung airways, tissue and the circulatory or lymphatic system.

Most metal and metalloid ions are relatively nonvolatile at room temperature. Mercury is volatile in the pure metal form, but only a few ionic forms of mercury are volatile at temperatures less than 100 °C. The temperature of tobacco burning at the tip of a cigarette may reach over 900 °C. Smoke inhaled into the mouth (mainstream smoke) is at approximately 30 °C, and the temperature of sidestream smoke leaving the burning tip falls below 100 °C about 10 cm from the tip (*30*). Thus, a burning cigarette tip is hot enough to volatilize many metal ions or to cause them to react with other substances to form volatile compounds and complexes. As a consequence, some metals may be present in the gas phase in metallic or compound form, whereas others may condense into a particulate phase of the smoke. Although the exact composition depends on individual smoking habits, a puff of cigarette smoke might consist of approximately 70% air, 17% gas phase species, 8% particulate matter and 5% miscellaneous components (*31*). By the time the smoke is inhaled or rises in a plume from the cigarette as sidestream smoke, most of the metal ions are condensed with other materials, forming aerosol particles, which comprise much of the particulate matter of the smoke aerosol (*30*).

Cigarette smoke is a major source of exposure to ultrafine and fine particulate matter. Most of the particulate mass occurs in particles with diameters of 0.1–1.3 μm, the lower half of the fine particle diameter range (*32,33*). Although ultrafine particulate from tobacco smoke is not the particulate fraction with the greatest mass, its small size facilitates uptake into cells, and it is much more toxic and induces more oxidative stress per unit mass because of its greater surface area-to-mass ratio (*34*).

Exposure to a given toxic metal or metalloid is limited by its concentration in the tobacco product. Therefore, the concentrations of metals and metalloids in tobacco are proportional to the amounts transported in smoke from combustion products (*7–9*). Analysis of toxic metals in tobacco is easier because the concentrations are higher than in smoke and a smoking machine is not required. Although many studies on metals in tobacco (cigarette filler) have been published, many poorly describe the analytical methods used and provide little or no information for evaluating the accuracy of the method; few describe proper calibration, use of certified standards or certified or standard reference tobacco or other leaf, which are necessary to assure the accuracy or quality of the data. This annex includes the most recent reports of metal concentrations in tobacco in which at least a minimal effort was made to demonstrate analytical accuracy, with a few exceptions. This overview should therefore not be construed as exhaustive or comprehensive.

In most published reports of metal concentrations in cigarette smoke, standardized machine smoking regimens were used, based on the standard ISO conditions (35-ml puff volume, 2-s puff duration, 60-s puff frequency). Few results have been obtained under intense smoking conditions (50-ml puff volume, 2-s puff duration, 30-s puff frequency with any ventilation holes blocked).

Once a metal or metalloid is absorbed into the lung, its fate determines much of its health impact. Metals such as cadmium and chromium may accumulate and remain predominantly in lung tissue for a long biological lifetime (*35*), although some may be trapped in mucus, coughed up and swallowed. Second-hand smoke from cigarettes is a source of exposure to toxic substances for people in an unventilated room with a smoker. It is also possible that people in close proximity to a smoker, such as small children held close to the smoker, might be exposed to low concentrations of toxic substances, including aluminium, cadmium, lead and other metals, that are exhaled in moist aerosols for some time after smoking (*36*).

Selected biological and public health effects of metals

Dose–response relations

A dose–response relation is a mathematical characterization of the effect on an organism of exposure to a chemical, radiation or other stressor. The characterization may be made on the basis of various levels of exposure for a specific duration. If the duration is relatively short, it is described as 'acute' exposure. The corollary is that, at a given level of exposure, the dose–response relation depends on the duration of exposure. If the duration of exposure is relatively long or repeated frequently, it may be described as 'chronic'. The biological response to exposure to a stressor therefore depends on both the level and duration of exposure. The response to acute exposure may not be proportionally the same as the response to chronic exposure.

Examples of biological responses to both acute and chronic exposures to toxic metals as a consequence of the use of tobacco products and as a consequence of occupational exposures are given below. In many cases, the consequences of short, low-level, chronic exposure would not be expected to result in all the pathological manifestations of acute high-level exposure, nor to the same intensity. Thus, some of the consequences of exposure to metals discussed below may not be due to lower chronic exposure to toxic metals in tobacco products. Other factors that must be considered, however, when evaluating the effects of exposure to toxic metals are bioaccumulation and sensitization. Although a single acute exposure or low-level chronic exposure may not result in clinical effects, bioaccumulation may increase the pathological response over time. Several metals and metalloids described below bioaccumulate in the lung and other tissues as a consequence of tobacco use. If a tissue is sensitized to a metal, a biological response will often subsequently be observed at much lower concentrations. Several metals described below are known to be potent sensitizers, and some of them also bioaccumulate.

Aluminium

A working group convened by the IARC found sufficient evidence for the carcinogenicity to humans of certain exposures occurring during aluminium production (group 1), although this does not apply to all exposure to aluminium (*37*). Occupational exposure to aluminium in some chemical forms has occasionally been reported to result in chronic bronchitis, aluminium pneumoconiosis, pulmonary fibrosis and granulomatosis, and anaphylactic responses (*38–41*). Aluminium has been shown to be toxic to lung, bone and nervous tissue in experimental animals. Sensitivity to the toxicity of aluminium may be age-dependent in humans, children being the most vulnerable (*42*).

Aluminium has been found at significantly higher concentrations in the exhaled breath condensate of patients with chronic obstructive pulmonary disease (COPD) than that of nonsmoking healthy controls. When the COPD patients who were smokers were compared with ex-smokers and nonsmokers, they had statistically significantly higher concentrations of aluminium in exhaled breath condensate (*36*).

Selected results of analyses of aluminium concentrations in smokeless tobacco and cigarette filler tobacco are summarized in Tables 1 and 2.

Arsenic

Arsenic is an IARC group 1 human carcinogen (*52*). It is extensively absorbed after oral or inhalation intake, and, depending on the route of exposure, can cause lung cancer, skin cancer, dermal sensitization and cardiovascular effects. It is difficult to correlate exposure to arsenic with levels measured during biomonitoring, as arsenic is rapidly cleared from the blood, with a half-life of 3–4 h. Excretion in urine is also transient (*53*).

In an epidemiological study of arsenic-induced skin lesions in an area of Bangladesh where well-water has high arsenic concentrations, 157 women

Table 1. Concentrations of metals and yields of extractable metals reported in smokeless tobacco (µg/g tobacco)

Metal	Country (reference)							
	Ghana (*43*)	Canada (*27*)	India (*44–46*)	USA (*47*)	USA (*26*)	Artificial saliva[a] (*26*)	Phosphate[a] (*25*)	DTPA, EDTA or EDDHA[a] (*25*)
Al	3006–5167	NR	NR	NR	NR	NR	NR	NR
As	0.108–0.256	0.143–0.437	0.1–3.5	NR	0.13–0.29	NR	NR	NR
Ba	110–203	NR	NR	NR	38–158	3.1–19 (3–21%)	NR	NR
Be	NR	NR	NR	NR	0.010–0.038	< 0.003–0.010 (21–32%)	NR	NR
Cd	1.06–1.11	0.30–1.09	0.1–3.1	0.73–1.58	0.66–1.88	0.302–0.508 (21–47%)	5–15%	81–109%
Co	0.056–0.201	NR	NR	NR	0.26–1.22	0.171–0.739 (30–65%)	NR	NR
Cr	0.95–1.41	0.71–2.19	5.25–21.9	NR	0.86–3.20	NR	NR	NR
Cu	18.5–27.7	NR	9.02–61.5	NR	NR	NR	24–39%	23–54%
Fe	2433–6982	NR	354–3213	NR	NR	NR	NR	NR
Hg	0.007–0.012	NR	0.02–0.11	NR	NR	NR	NR	NR
Mn	121–139							
Ni	NR	0.84–2.05	1.33–13.1	NR	1.39–2.73	0.370–1.153 (30–46%)	0–2.5%	15–64%
Pb	NR	0.23–1.20	1.76–13	0.27–2.96	0.28–0.85	< 0.13–0.153 (8%)	NR	NR

DTPA, diethylene triamine pentaacetic acid; EDTA, ethylenediaminetetraacetic acid; DDHA, dihexylhexanamide; NR, not reported

[a] Extractable metals from smokeless tobacco (µg/g tobacco)

Table 2. Concentrations of metals reported in cigarette tobacco (μg/g tobacco)

Metal	Country (reference)					
	Canada (*8*)	India (*46*)	Pakistan (*48*)	United Kingdom (*49*)	USA (*50*)	USA (*51*)
Al	NR	NR	431–782	NR	699–1200	NR
As	0.151	NR	0.73–0.86	0.1–0.7	NR	0.250–0.250
Ba	NR	NR	NR	NR	40.7–56.6	68.3–75.1
Be	NR	NR	NR	NR	NR	0.016–0.017
Cd	0.930	0.28–0.87	2.2–4.5	0.5–0.8	NR	NR
Co	NR	NR	NR	NR	< 0.01–0.94	0.348–0.425
Cr	0.353	2.8–5.0	NR	1.3–3.1	NR	0.484–1.27
Cu	NR	9.01–19.2	NR	11.7–16.2	NR	3.49–4.00
Fe	NR	468–1129	NR	293–576	NR	NR
Hg	0.027	NR	NR	NR	NR	0.020–0.021
Mn	NR	NR	NR	NR	155–400	NR
Ni	0.250	7.21–10.2	1.2–2.8	1.1–2.7	NR	1.13–1.18
Pb	0.257	0.79–5.79	1.1–1.6	0.4–0.9	NR	0.604–0.607

who chewed tobacco had statistically significantly higher levels of urinary methylarsonic acid metabolite than 352 who did not use tobacco (at the 99% confidence interval). The median total urinary arsenic of women who chewed tobacco was 20 µg/l higher than that of those who did not use tobacco, although the difference was not statistically significant. The mean odds ratios for arsenic-induced skin lesions among women who used chewing tobacco as compared with those who did not were 3.8 for those with urinary methylarsonic acid in the lowest tertile and 7.3 and 7.5 for those with urinary methylarsonic acid or inorganic arsenic in the highest tertile, respectively (*54*). Although arsenic in water can be considered the cause of the skin lesions, smokeless tobacco products appeared to potentiate this endpoint. Biologically available arsenic from the tobacco products was not considered to be the sole cause of the increased incidence, but it is possible that arsenic in the products and other toxic substances contributed. In this study, the mean odds ratios for skin lesions in male cigarette smokers (only two were female) were 4.1 for those who did not use tobacco in any form and 2.3 for those who used chewing tobacco in comparison with people who did not use tobacco in any form. Both were statistically significant.

Selected results of analyses of arsenic concentrations in smokeless tobacco and cigarette tobacco are summarized in Tables 1 and 2. Selected results of analyses of arsenic concentrations in cigarette smoke particulate obtained with ISO and Health Canada Intense smoking regimens are summarized in Table 3.

Barium

The best-known toxic effect of barium is hypokalaemia, as barium is a potassium channel antagonist, which blocks the passive efflux of intracellular potassium. When ingested orally or inhaled, barium can cause tachycardia, hypertension and granulomatous pneumoconiosis. Barium is also a dermal chemical irritant and may cause dermal lesions, depending on the exposure concentration (*57,58*).

Selected results of analyses of barium concentrations in smokeless tobacco and cigarette tobacco are summarized in Tables 1 and 2. One study in which artificial saliva was used to mimic human uptake of extractable barium in smokeless tobacco showed that it was readily extracted (*26*). Although the extraction efficiency from smokeless tobacco shown in Table 1 was low in some cases, the net mass of artificial saliva-extractable barium was the highest of all the metals examined.

Beryllium

Beryllium is an IARC group 1 human carcinogen (*59*). It is also known to cause inflammation and sensitization reactions after dermal or inhalation

Table 3. Concentrations of metals reported in cigarette smoke (μg/cigarette)

Metal	Smoking regimen (reference)				
	Phillip Morris International ISO (*55*)	Phillip Morris International Intense (*55*)	Canada ISO (*8*)	Canada Intense (*8*)	USA ISO (*56*)
As	< LOD–0.0055	< LOD–0.0145			
Cd	0.0016–0.101	0.0435–0.1971	0.0576	0.1608	0.0138–0.0624
Hg	0.0011–0.0063	0.0042–0.0107	0.0032	0.0065	
Pb	0.0039–0.0392	0.0257–0.0932	0.0167	0.0372	0.0071–0.0289

LOD, limit of detection

exposure. Chronic pulmonary exposure may result in the granulomatous and fibrotic lung disease, berylliosis, which further presents with interstitial oedema and progresses to fibrotic obstructive disease (*60*).

Because the concentration of beryllium in tobacco, and consequently in smoke particulate, is lower than those of other metals, its concentration in tobacco smoke is generally below the detection limit of analytical methods. The concentrations of beryllium in tobacco smoke reported in the literature have been tabulated (*61*); however, examination of the original references reveals that the reported concentrations in cigarette smoke were the limits of detection of the methods cited. Thus, it is difficult to assess the significance to health of beryllium in tobacco smoke. In a study of beryllium sensitization and chronic beryllium disease in a beryllium machining plant, 20 of 235 people with a lifetime weighted average airborne exposure of 0.024–0.6 $\mu g/m^3$, well below the 2 $\mu g/m^3$ occupational exposure limit intended to prevent chronic beryllium disease, were found to be sensitized to beryllium (*62*). Sensitization occurs after both pulmonary and dermal exposure. Once sensitization is detectable, the obstructive disease progresses at a rate depending on the level of exposure (*63*).

Beryllium sulfate is an insoluble ionic form, as is the oxide. Beryllium ion in poorly soluble form tends to accumulate in the lung to a concentration plateau, when equilibrium is reached between deposition and clearance during continuous exposure. About half the concentration is cleared rapidly, predominantly via the lymphatic system, while the more slowly cleared portion may remain in the lungs for longer and be involved in toxic challenge. Exposed female rats had less efficient clearance and earlier morbidity and mortality than unexposed animals (*64*). Rhoades and Sanders (*65*) reported a 400-day half-life for clearance of beryllium oxide from rat lung. Thus, inflammation due to beryllium may be a concern for people who smoke or use smokeless tobacco.

Selected results of analyses of beryllium concentrations in smokeless tobacco and cigarette tobacco are summarized in Tables 1 and 2; however, the concentrations reported in the original references were the limits of detection for the methods cited (*61*). Extraction from smokeless tobacco into artificial saliva resulted in a measurable concentration of extractable beryllium for only one brand of moist snuff and three samples of leaf tobacco sold for chewing in the United States. The other four had less than 0.003 µg/g extractable beryllium (the limit of detection; *26*). The extraction efficiency for beryllium was higher than that for barium.

Cadmium

Cadmium is an IARC group 1 human carcinogen (*59*). It is highly toxic to kidney, bone and the nervous, respiratory and circulatory systems (*66*), and its accumulation in the lens is associated with cataracts (*67–69*). Increased blood cadmium levels are strongly associated with an increased prevalence of peripheral artery disease (*70*). Cadmium occurs at among the highest concentrations of all the toxic and carcinogenic metals in tobacco, and, once absorbed, it is not quickly excreted, with a biological half-life of 13.6–23.5 years (*71*), and bioaccumulates over time (*72*). As a consequence, cadmium is one of the most commonly studied metals in tobacco (*22,73–76*).

Cadmium competes with zinc for biological binding sites. The serum and prostate tissue cadmium-to-zinc ratios in healthy men and those with benign prostatic hypertrophy were always lower than those in men with prostate cancer (*77*). Kazi et al. (*78*) reported statistically significantly higher blood and scalp hair cadmium and lower zinc concentrations (at the 99.9% confidence interval) in male patients with oral cancer than in ‘referents’. They further reported that users of chewing tobacco with areca nut or betel quid had higher blood and scalp hair cadmium and lower zinc concentrations than those who did not use chewing tobacco. The same was true of tobacco smokers, for whom the cadmium-to-zinc ratios were even higher. Exposure to tobacco smoke is associated with elevated exposure to cadmium, reflected by elevated urine cadmium concentrations (*72*).

Associations have been reported between increased urinary cadmium concentration and periodontal disease (*79*); exposure to cadmium, smoking and pancreatic cancer (*80*); and exposure to cadmium, smoking and diabetes (*81*). Increased cadmium levels in lung tissue have been correlated with smoking history, showing that cadmium in some form reaches the lung (*35*). Tissue cadmium concentrations were statistically significantly higher in four of five lobes of smokers’ lungs than in those of nonsmokers, and the mean cadmium concentration was higher in the remaining lobe of smokers than of nonsmokers, although the difference was not statistically significant (*82*).

Elevated cadmium levels in body fat (*83*), blood (*84–86*), urine (*72,84,87*) and amniotic fluid (*85,88*) have been attributed to smoking or exposure to second-hand smoke, indicating systemic absorption from the lungs.

Pulmonary exposure to nebulized cadmium compounds was shown to induce emphysema (*89*). Cadmium has been found at higher concentrations in the exhaled breath condensate of people with COPD than that of nonsmoking healthy controls and at higher concentrations in current control smokers than control nonsmokers. When the COPD patients who were smokers were compared with ex-smokers and nonsmokers, they had statistically significantly higher concentrations of cadmium in exhaled breath condensate. The concentration of cadmium in exhaled breath condensate positively correlated with smoking history in pack-years (*36*).

Selected results of analyses of cadmium concentrations in smokeless tobacco and cigarette tobacco are summarized in Tables 1 and 2. One study in which artificial saliva was used to mimic human uptake of extractable cadmium in smokeless tobacco showed that cadmium was readily extracted. The results, with extraction efficiency, are shown in Table 1. The Table also includes extraction efficiency values from Maier et al. (*25*), who used phosphate buffer or 0.001 mol/l of the chelating agents dihexylhexanamide (DHHA), EDTA and DTPA in phosphate buffer. Selected results of analyses of cadmium concentrations in cigarette smoke particulate obtained with ISO and Health Canada Intense smoking regimens are summarized in Table 3.

Normalization of the cadmium deliveries from United States cigarettes to tar delivery eliminated all significant differences between smoke delivery categories (*56*). Differences in delivery can therefore be attributed to differences in filter ventilation levels. The levels of cadmium transported in smoke particulate matter from 21 counterfeits of two popular United States brands seized in 2003 in six length and nominal smoke delivery categories were 2.0–6.5 times higher than in the authentic brands purchased in 2003, and the differences were all significant (*90*). Stephens et al. (*91*) reported significantly higher cadmium concentrations in tobacco from counterfeit cigarettes seized in the United Kingdom than in authentic brands.

Chromium

Chromium [VI] is an IARC group 1 human carcinogen (*59*). It also causes oral and epidermal allergic contact dermatitis and pulmonary sensitization (*92–97*). As chromium [VI] is found in cigarette smoke and ash (*98*), it is not clear whether all chromium [VI] is formed during combustion or whether some is already present in tobacco as a consequence of absorption from soil.

Although chromium [III] is required nutritionally at low concentrations, some reports indicate that high exposure might also result in contact allergic sensitization (*95*). Sógor et al. (*98*) reported chromium [VI] in cigarette ash and found that chromium [III] was quantitatively oxidized to chromium [VI] when ashed at 800 °C in a muffle furnace, although digestion in acid reduced it to chromium [III]. Most chromium [VI] was found in the ash. While it is generally presumed that most of the chromium in tobacco is in the chromium [III] oxidation state (*98*), manganese oxides are known to oxidize chromium [III] to chromium [VI] in soil and solutions (*99*). As manganese in one or more oxidation states is transported in smoke particulate matter, it might also occur at some level in saliva, in moist smoke particulate droplets and on moist surfaces in the lungs.

Accumulation of chromium in lung tissue has been correlated with smoking history, confirming that it reaches the lung in some form (*35*). The concentrations of chromium in excised tissue from smokers' lungs were significantly higher than in nonsmokers' lungs in all five lobes examined (*82*). It is not clear, however, in what proportions chromium [III] and chromium [VI] accumulate. The studies to date have been based on analyses by difference, giving some confidence that the results actually do show chromium [VI] formation and possible transport in smoke particulate. Derivation of a result by differences between analyses of separate components or the results of separate analytical procedures is often used as a substitute when a method for direct measurement is not available. Chromium in tobacco smoke is therefore a health concern, but it is currently difficult to determine the full health consequences of oral, pulmonary and systemic exposure in view of insufficient characterization of the oxidation state of chromium.

Selected results of analyses of chromium concentrations in smokeless tobacco and cigarette tobacco are summarized in Tables 1 and 2.

Copper

Copper is required nutritionally at low concentrations. Inhaled copper is a respiratory irritant, causing alveolar migration of macrophages, eosinophilia, formation of histiocytic and noncaseating granulomas containing copper inclusions, pulmonary fibrosis, and formation of fibrohyaline nodules similar to those found in silicosis as a consequence of high industrial inhalation exposure (*100*). Copper is an oxidation–reduction (redox) active metal, as is iron. As iron is found at higher concentrations in tobacco than is copper, the relevance of redox activity is discussed only for iron.

Although copper has been reported at significantly lower concentrations in the exhaled breath condensate of people with COPD than that of nonsmoking healthy controls (*36*), it has been found at statistically significantly higher concentrations in the blood of smokers than of nonsmokers (*101*).

Selected results of analyses of copper concentrations in smokeless tobacco and cigarette tobacco are summarized in Tables 1 and 2. Table 1 also shows the extraction efficiency with phosphate buffer or 0.001 mol/l of the chelating agents DHHA, EDTA and DTPA in phosphate buffer.

Iron

Iron is required nutritionally at low concentrations; however, it is known to catalyse highly reactive hydroxyl radical formation from superoxide ion and hydrogen peroxide by the two-step Fenton reaction (*102*). As a consequence, inhaled iron contributes to free radical-induced lung injury.

Thompson et al. (*103*) found that the intracellular iron burdens in both bronchial and alveolar lavage samples from asymptomatic smokers and smokers with chronic bronchitis were much higher than those of nonsmoking study participants. The extracellular iron burden of alveolar lavage samples from people with chronic bronchitis was also higher than that of nonsmokers. Alveolar macrophages act to diminish heavy lung iron burdens by taking up extracellular free iron and sequestering iron [III] bound to ferritin and, to a lesser degree, transferrin. As the intracellular iron burden increases, iron-saturated ferritin precipitates intracellularly in the form of haemosiderin. Wesselius, Nelson and Skikne (*104*) showed that iron-loaded alveolar macrophages from light and heavy smokers released higher concentrations of both iron and soluble ferritin in vitro than did macrophages from nonsmokers. Moreno et al. (*105*) showed the physiological relevance of iron and ferritin release from alveolar macrophages by demonstrating that aqueous extracts of cigarette smoke could reduce iron [III] and cause its release from ferritin. Addition of superoxide dismutase increased the rate of iron release. Boyer, Clarke and LaRoche (*106*) modelled the effects of polycyclic hydroxy aromatic compounds in cigarette smoke and found that plant phenolics cause reduction and release of ferritin iron. Ghio et al. (*107*) found that the concentrations of iron, ferritin, serum ferritin and non-haem iron in lung and liver increased after exposure of rats to cigarette smoke. Iron has been reported at statistically significantly lower concentrations in the exhaled breath condensate of people with COPD than that of nonsmoking healthy controls (*36*), but Padmavathi et al. (*108*) found iron at statistically significantly higher concentrations in the serum of long-term smokers than of nonsmokers, in agreement with the findings in rats and humans of Ghio et al. (*107*). These studies demonstrate that potentiation of iron oxidation–reduction chemistry contributes to the oxidative stress and damage in the lung caused by smoking.

The presence of traces of iron in particulate has been shown to augment the pulmonary inflammatory response to silica (*109–112*).

Selected results of analyses of iron concentrations in smokeless tobacco and cigarette tobacco are summarized in Tables 1 and 2.

Lead

Lead is an IARC group 2A probable human carcinogen (*113*). It is also highly neurotoxic, and low levels of exposure to lead are associated with detrimental prenatal neurological and other developmental effects. Even in adults, blood lead concentrations considered to be acceptably low (< 10 µg/dl) have been associated with raised systemic blood pressure and reduced glomerular filtration rate (*114*). Lead accumulates over a lifetime in bone. Although bone lead concentrations are more closely correlated with its pathological effects, few results are available for bone, because obtaining such samples is more invasive than obtaining blood or urine.

Tissue lead concentrations were statistically significantly higher in four of five lobes of smokers' lungs than in those of nonsmokers; although the mean lead concentration was higher in the remaining lobe of smokers than of nonsmokers, the difference was not statistically significant (*82*). Lead accumulation in blood and amniotic fluid from women (*85*) and in cord blood from newborns (*115,116*) has been associated with smoking, and high blood lead levels in children in the United States were associated with exposure to second-hand smoke (*117*).

Lead has been reported at higher concentrations in the exhaled breath condensate of people with COPD than that of nonsmoking controls and at higher concentrations in that of current normal smokers than in that of nonsmokers. When the COPD patients who smoked were compared with ex-smokers and nonsmokers, they had statistically significantly higher concentrations of lead in exhaled breath condensate (*36*).

Normalization of the lead delivery in the smoke of United States cigarettes to that of tar eliminated all the statistically significant differences between smoke delivery categories; however, although the differences between full flavour and ultralight smoke delivery categories in the nicotine-normalized concentration of lead in smoke particulate were still significant, they were not statistically significantly different for full flavour and ultra-light or light and ultra-light categories. A comparison of lead concentrations in identical varieties purchased in 2004 were not statistically significantly different from the comparable 2002 varieties of the brands tested, with one exception (*56*). The lead in mainstream smoke particulate matter from 21 counterfeits of two popular United States brands seized in 2003 in six different length and nominal smoke delivery categories were 3.0–13.8 times higher than in the authentic brands purchased in 2003, and the differences were statistically significant (*90*). Stephens et al. (*49*) reported significantly higher lead concentrations in tobacco from counterfeit cigarettes seized in the United Kingdom than in authentic brands.

Selected results of analyses of the lead concentrations in smokeless tobacco and cigarette tobacco are summarized in Tables 1 and 2. One study in which artificial saliva was used to mimic human uptake of extractable lead in smokeless tobacco showed that lead was not readily extracted (*26*). The results, including extraction efficiency values, are shown in Table 1. Selected results of analyses of lead concentrations in cigarette smoke particulate obtained with ISO and Health Canada Intense smoking regimens are summarized in Table 3.

Manganese

Although manganese is required nutritionally at low concentrations, it is neurotoxic at high concentrations. The symptoms of neurotoxicity may not be observed immediately but often become clinically detectable with long-term exposure (*118*). Leikauff (*119*) cited United States Environmental Protection Agency reports that compounds of manganese are suspected of inducing or exacerbating asthma.

The commonest oxidation states of manganese are its +2, +3, +4, +6 and +7 states (manganese [II], [III], [IV], [VI] or [VII]), although its +5 oxidation state is also observed as a consequence of disproportionation from the +4 and +6 states. Manganese [II] is the most stable oxidation state (*120*) and one of the states involved in the Mn [III]–Mn [II] redox cycle of manganese as a cofactor in metalloenzymes, such as human superoxide dismutase. Manganese [II] complexes have been found in tobacco (*121*). Although manganese [II] is typically found at higher concentrations than other metals, it is less frequently reported in studies of tobacco products because it is difficult to analyse. Manganese [IV] is less common in biological systems but exists in complex-bound forms, such as plant photosystem II proteins (*122*) and some bacterial systems in which manganese is enzymatically oxidized (*123,124*). The [III] and [IV] oxidation states are generally more toxic, as are other higher oxidation states in uncomplexed forms. The manganese [III], [IV], [V], [VI] and [VII] oxidation states are strongly oxidizing: in soil, manganese oxides oxidize chromium [III] to chromium [VI] (*99*). More studies are needed to elucidate the complex relations between tobacco, manganese oxidation and metabolism in tobacco smoke, circulation, brain uptake and neurological effects.

Matusch et al. (*125*) showed that manganese is concentrated in the medial hypothalamus, the nucleus ruber, the accessory oculomotor nucleus and the substantia nigra in normal mouse brain. Reaney et al. (*126*) showed that manganese [II] accumulates in whole rat brain, but Gómez et al. (*127*) found that the manganese concentrations in whole rat brain decreased with length of exposure to very high aluminium concentrations. Cigarette smoke transports both aluminium and manganese, and Uz et al. (*128*) reported that the serum manganese level was generally lower in smokers than nonsmokers. The poorly characterized nature of the relation between use of tobacco products, circulating manganese concentrations and possible interactions between manganese and other metals with regard to neurotoxicity requires further investigation.

Bast-Pettersen and Ellingsen (*129*), in a generally well-designed study, found increased tremor among smokers exposed occupationally to manganese as compared with nonsmokers. They could distinguish clinically between the tremor attributable to manganese alone and smokers' tremor.

Selected results of analyses of manganese concentrations in smokeless tobacco and cigarette tobacco are summarized in Tables 1 and 2.

Mercury

Mercury is not generally considered to be carcinogenic, but it is strongly toxic to the reproductive and nervous systems in its metallic, organic and inorganic forms (*6,130*). Mercury from dental amalgam is associated with sensitization and intraoral lichenoid lesions in some cases (*131,132*). Metallic mercury and mercury compounds were included on a list of 33 air pollutants of concern because of their toxicity and as respiratory tract irritants that might exacerbate asthma (*119*).

Selected results of analyses of mercury concentrations in smokeless tobacco and cigarette tobacco are summarized in Tables 1 and 2. Selected results of analyses of mercury concentrations in cigarette smoke particulate obtained with ISO and Health Canada Intense smoking regimens are summarized in Table 3.

Nickel and cobalt

Although both cobalt and nickel are required nutritionally at trace concentrations, nickel is an IARC group 1 human carcinogen (*133*), and cobalt is an IARC group 2B possible human carcinogen (*134,135*). The two metals are discussed together because, although cobalt is not considered as potent a carcinogen as nickel and is not generally present in tobacco at concentrations as high as those of nickel, they both cause immunological sensitization, including epidermal and oral allergic contact sensitization, contact dermatitis, pulmonary inflammation, pneumoconioses and asthma (*93,96,97,136–138*). Once a person is sensitized to one of these metals, immunological cross-sensitization to the other is often observed, as they share an endothelial inflammatory activation pathway (*136,139–141*). Although lipopolysaccharide is the natural ligand for human Toll-like receptor 4, which is involved in the inflammatory response, nickel [II] directly activates proinflammatory signal cascades by binding to this receptor (*142*). Dolovich, Evans and Nieboer (*143*) identified an additional mechanism by which nickel sensitization-induced inflammation occurs: binding to the copper-binding site of human serum albumin and sensitization to the resulting metal–protein complex. Cobalt could compete for nickel binding to serum albumin and to the antibody complex.

Tissue nickel concentrations were reported to be significantly higher in all five lobes of smokers' lungs than in nonsmokers' lungs (*82*). Nickel has been found in significantly higher concentrations in placenta samples from smokers than in those from nonsmokers (*88*), indicating probable systemic absorption from the lungs.

Selected results of analyses of cobalt and nickel concentrations in smokeless tobacco and cigarette tobacco are summarized in Tables 1 and 2. One study in which artificial saliva was used to mimic human uptake of extractable cobalt and nickel from smokeless tobacco showed that both were readily extracted (*26*). The results for extraction efficiency are shown in Table 1, with the values for phosphate buffer and 0.001 mol/l of the chelating agents DHHA, EDTA and DTPA in phosphate buffer.

Polonium-210 and lead-210

Polonium has been shown to be transported in tobacco smoke (*144,145*). Calculations by Desideri et al. (*146*) based on minimal filter retention of polonium-210 and lead-210 from cigarette smoke suggested that smoking could provide a considerable portion of the whole dose resulting from avoidable exposure to natural radioactivity.

Polonium-210 and lead-210, radioactive daughters of radon, are IARC group 1 human carcinogens (*147*). Polonium-210 is the only polonium isotopic descendant of radon with a half-life greater than 1 s (138 days). Lead-210 is predominantly a β-radiation emitter and the only lead isotopic descendant with a half-life greater than 11 h (22.26 years). Thus, these isotopes are the only radioactive isotopes of polonium and lead that can feasibly be studied in tobacco or smoke. The α-radiation emitted by polonium-210 consists of very high-energy particles and is therefore an ionizing, mutagenic threat to epithelial, lung and other tissues after absorption. As a result, polonium-210 accounts for the largest proportion of the health threat associated with exposure to radon and its daughters. Although they are found at low concentrations in tobacco smoke, polonium-210 and lead-210 are severe health concerns (*147,148*).

Selected results of analyses of polonium-210 and lead-210 concentrations in smokeless tobacco and cigarette tobacco are summarized in Table 4. The concentrations extractable from smokeless tobacco in human saliva are also summarized in Table 4. Calculations of exposure based on the deliveries of polonium-210 and lead-210 in smoke from Chinese cigarettes showed that cigarette smoking is the main source of exposure to these radioactive metals for people who smoke.

Silicon

Silicon is taken up from soil by plants in the available form, generally as kaolin (aluminium silicate). Kaolin accumulates in higher plants and appears to have both structural and stress resistance roles in plant physiology (*154*). The concentration of silicate in plants exceeds its solubility, and it forms biogenic 'phytoliths' (*155*), which are predominantly silica (SiO_2) polymers.

Crystalline silica inhaled in the form of quartz or cristobalite (forms of SiO_2) is an IARC group 1 human carcinogen (*156*). When tobacco smoke is inhaled, it carries with it silicates in the form of aluminium silicate and silica particles, and aluminium silicate particles are found in smokers' lungs at high concentrations (*157*). Lynn et al. (*158*) reported that bronchoalveolar lavage samples from a patient with pulmonary disease contained 10^{11} black macrophages with prominent lysosomes containing amorphous carbon, round dense particles and needle-like crystals of aluminium silicate, for which no source except smoking was found. Choux et al. (*159*) described the composition of numerous silicate particles in alveolar macrophages from a patient with tobacco-associated pulmonary fibrosis as fibre-, needle- or laminar-like inclusions measuring 0.2–2 µm. Aluminium and silicon were the major elemental components, corresponding to the composition of kaolinite; iron and sulfur were also found. Brody and Craighead (*160*) described lysosomal 'smokers inclusions' in interstitial and alveolar macrophages and lymphocytes as consisting predominantly of aluminium silicate with plate-like structures and suggested their involvement in pulmonary fibrosis. Heckman and Lehman (*161*) reported that rat lung epithelial cells exposed chronically to tobacco smoke contained elongated cytoplasmic inclusions. Macrophages had similar but larger inclusions composed of silicon, aluminium, phosphorus, iron and sulfur. Thus, silicate metal-bearing particulate is a major component of the particulate found in smokers' lungs. As described above, the presence of traces of iron augments the pulmonary inflammatory response to

Table 4. Polonium-210 and lead-210 concentrations in mBq/g tobacco and deliveries from smokeless and cigarette tobacco

Tobacco product	Country (reference)						
	USA (*47*)	USA (*149*)	Brazil (*150*)	Greece (*152*)	Greece (*152*)	Italy (*146*)	China (*153*)
Smokeless tobacco							
Polonium-210	5.9–24	NR	NR	NR	NR	NR	NR
Lead-210	NR	NR	NR	NR	NR	NR	NR
Saliva-extractable							
Polonium-210	NR	8.7–13.9	NR	NR	NR	NR	NR
Lead-210	NR	8.6–13.6	NR	NR	NR	NR	NR
Cigarette tobacco							
Polonium-210	NR	NR	10.9–27.4	NR	3.6–17.0	6.84–17.49	18–29
Lead-210	NR	NR	11.9–30.2	6.3–18.2	7.3–16.7	NR	17–24
Intake from smoke (mBq/cigarette)							
Polonium-210	NR	NR	NR	NR	NR	NR	3.0
Lead-210	NR	NR	NR	NR	NR	NR	1.85

NR, not reported

silica (*109–112*). Nonsmokers may also be exposed to environmental silica but to a much lower extent, unless they are exposed occupationally to high concentrations (*162*).

Silicon in tobacco or smoke is difficult to analyse on many instruments. Rhoades and White (*163*) reported levels of < 0.07–0.39 μg/cigarette of silicon in particulate matter transported in smoke from three different cigarettes, including a 1R4F reference cigarette and one light and one ultralight cigarette smoked under 'extreme' conditions.

Possible involvement of metals in oral inflammation after use of smokeless tobacco

Exposure to some of the metals discussed above in relation to tobacco consumption causes adverse health effects other than carcinogenicity. Beryllium, chromium, cobalt, mercury and nickel, as discussed earlier, are known to cause sensitization, resulting in allergic contact inflammation. Oral exposure to some metals can also affect health. In particular, oral sensitization to cobalt, nickel, mercury and other metals in dental materials has been shown to result in allergic contact stomatitis, joint pain, positive allergic skin patch tests to the metals and other systemic manifestations in some people (*132*). Amini et al. (*164*) showed that the concentrations of nickel in oral mucosal cells of patients with fixed orthodontic appliances were statistically significantly higher than in people without such appliances. Their results demonstrated that oral exposure to nickel is not only superficial, but that the mucosal cells absorb nickel from saliva.

Kazi et al. (*78*) reported statistically significantly higher blood and scalp hair cadmium and lower zinc concentrations in male oral cancer patients than in 'referents'. Furthermore, users of chewing tobacco with areca nut or betel quid had higher blood and scalp hair cadmium and lower zinc concentrations than people who did not use chewing tobacco. In a separate study, similar findings were reported for female mouth cancer patients (*167*). These studies indicate that oral or alimentary absorption of cadmium from smokeless tobacco products results in high blood and hair cadmium-to-zinc ratios in smokeless tobacco consumers. These studies also illustrate the health risk due to cumulative absorption of a carcinogenic metal from smokeless tobacco or from tobacco smoke, whereas a single exposure (sometimes discussed as a means of minimizing health risks) would probably pose a minimal risk.

Some combination of irritants, toxins and allergens in smokeless tobacco causes the contact inflammation observed as a consequence of its use. The oral cavity has a lining of highly vascular mucosa, parts of which are uniquely sensitive to irritants that can penetrate the tissue easily (*166*). Metal sensitization or toxicity resulting from exposure to metals extracted by saliva from tobacco held close to oral tissues might contribute appreciably to the hyperkeratosis, leukoplakia, erythroplakia and other oral inflammatory lesions observed as a consequence of smokeless tobacco use, as the lesions caused by metals alone and by smokeless tobacco are similar. Additional evidence to support this possibility is the finding that the concentration and distribution of metallothionein in oral mucosa change with development of the dysplasia that is characteristically observed with leukoplakia. Cellular concentrations of metallothionein and its cellular and intracellular distribution from the superficial to the basal mucosal layers differ markedly in non-dysplastic oral mucosa and in moderate dysplasia observed with leukoplakia (*167*). In inflammation, the oral mucosa apparently protects itself from the binding of toxic metals to metallothionein. Feron et al. (*168*) and Mueller (*169*) described the risk for carcinogenesis resulting from chronic inflammation of various epithelial and mucosal tissues, whether the cause was irritant, allergic or other. Thus, chronic oral inflammation is a consequence of smokeless tobacco consumption due to acute or chronic exposure to metals alone or to metals in combination with other components.

Smoking, metals, inflammation and sensitization

Geiser et al. (*170*) exposed rat lung to 4–5 µg of insoluble ultrafine (< 0.1 µm) titanium oxide particles and found that the particles were widely distributed on the luminal sides of the airways and alveoli in all tissue compartments and cells and within capillaries. They concluded that the ultrafine particles were not taken up by endocytic processes but by diffusion. Ferin and Oberdörster (*171*), however, concluded that particles that are not phagocytized by alveolar macrophages are taken up by endocytosis in alveolar epithelial cells. They found that increasing the particle number (essentially a condition of particle overload) or increasing particle size promoted interstitialization associated with inflammation. Therefore, particle dose, size and composition (discussed below) may affect the response and clearance mechanism to some degree. As discussed earlier, smaller particle size increases the potential for oxidative stress per unit mass of particulate matter as a consequence of the greater surface area-to-mass ratio of ultrafine particulate and its greater uptake and transcytosis by epithelial cells (*34*).

There is strong biochemical and pathological evidence that airway sensitization and inflammation, including atopic inflammation, are consequences of exposure to tobacco smoke particulate. There is growing evidence for a relation between exposure to mainstream and sidestream smoke and diseases resulting from oxidative challenge and inflammation, directly as a consequence of the activity of neutrophils, macrophages, dendritic cells, eosinophils and basophils and as a humoral immunological consequence of sensitization.

Rumold et al. (*174*) studied the sensitization of immunologically low-responder (C57BL/6) mice exposed to nebulized ovalbumin with and without concurrent inhalation of sidestream smoke. Exposure to sidestream smoke induced sensitization to ovalbumin, as seen from antigen-specific immunoglobulin E, whereas no detectable sensitization was seen in mice exposed to ovalbumin alone. Upon rechallenge, significantly increased levels of proinflammatory GM-CSF and IL-2 cytokines were detected in bronchoalveolar lavage samples, even in animals exposed to sidestream smoke alone.

Goel et al. (*175*) reported significantly higher serum immunoglobulin E concentrations in smokers than in ex-smokers and nonsmokers in a study of 70 people. The absolute eosinophil counts of smokers and ex-smokers did not differ significantly, but both were significantly higher than those of nonsmokers. No significant airway obstruction was measured in nonsmokers, but both smokers and ex-smokers had significantly greater obstruction than nonsmokers. Ex-smokers showed significantly more airways obstruction than current smokers.

Gilmour et al. (*176*) reported that intratracheal exposure of rats to residual oil fly ash particulate or its constituent metals (nickel and vanadium) caused significant pulmonary inflammation (increased protein levels and TNF-α, monocyte and granulocyte migration) and had an adjuvant effect on sensitization to dust mite, with immunoglobulin E production. Lambert et al. (*177*) showed that the enhanced sensitization was mediated by the soluble metal constituents of the particulate. Specifically, increased eosinophil numbers in bronchoalveolar lavage fluid were observed in response to either particulate or iron during sensitization. Dust mite-specific immunoglobulin E activity was greater in groups exposed to particulate, nickel or vanadium.

Carter et al. (*178*) studied the inflammatory effects of 5–200 µg/ml environmental particulate matter on normal human bronchial epithelial cells and found induction and expression of the pro-inflammatory cytokines TNF-α, IL-6 and IL-8. The particulate matter consisted of 2.6% carbon and hydrogen by mass, 18.8% vanadium, 3.75% nickel, 3.55% iron, and miscellaneous substances. Two hours after exposure, IL-6 and IL-8 mRNA was detected at significantly higher concentrations in cells exposed to 5 µg/ml particulate or more than in cells exposed to buffer alone. At 24 h, IL-8 protein was detected at a significantly higher level in cells exposed to 5 µg/ml particulate or more; IL-6 protein was found at a significantly higher level in cells exposed to 50 µg/ml particulate or more than in cells exposed to buffer alone. TNF-α mRNA was increased after a 2-h exposure to particulate at 50 µg/ml or more and TNF-α protein after 24 h. Cytokine production was inhibited by inclusion of the metal chelator deferoxamine. The authors concluded that metals present in particulate matter are responsible for inducing the production and release of inflammatory mediators by the respiratory tract.

Schaumann et al. (*179*) instilled suspensions of environmentally relevant concentrations of 100 µg of particulate matter ($PM_{2.5}$) collected in two German cities into contralateral lung segments of 12 healthy volunteers. Both instillations increased the numbers of leukocytes in bronchoalveolar lavage after 24 h, while the particulate matter from one city also significantly increased monocyte influx, TNF-α and IL-6 in lavage fluid and increased oxidant radical generation by the lavage cells. The authors concluded that the higher concentration of transition metals in $PM_{2.5}$ from the second city was responsible for the increased inflammation. The mean metal concentrations in the $PM_{2.5}$ suspension from this city were 692 µg/l zinc, 124 µg/l copper, 94 µg/l iron, 17 µg/l nickel, 9 µg/l vanadium, 8 µg/l lead, 3 µg/l chromium and 0.4 µg/l cadmium. Thus, the concentrations of metals that would be expected to induce inflammation were low.

Sanders et al. (*180*) showed that nickel [II] oxide and chromium [III] oxide dust particles were predominantly engulfed by alveolar macrophages in hamsters, with a smaller fraction in the alveolar lumen. A still smaller fraction was found in neutrophils of hamsters that were also exposed to cigarette smoke and in type I but not type II alveolar epithelium. The authors reported that neutrophils were rarely observed in the alveolar lumina of hamsters exposed only to nickel oxide and that vacuolization was more common in macrophages from animals also exposed to cigarette smoke. Alveolar macrophages may act as antigen-presenting cells. Regland et al. (*181*) reported a strong relation between smoking and nickel allergy.

The excessive lung burden of particulate iron as a consequence of smoking was examined in bronchoalveolar lavage samples from 27 healthy people, comprising nine nonsmokers, nine light smokers and nine heavy smokers (*104*). The authors recovered more than three times the number of macrophages from light smokers and more than eight times the number from heavy smokers than from nonsmokers. None of the nonsmokers had detectable iron (detection limit in lavage fluid, 10 ng/ml), whereas the mean iron concentration in fluid from light smokers was 12.5 ng/ml and that in lavage fluid from heavy smokers was 49.7 ng/ml. The authors found 7.7 times more ferritin in lavage fluid from light smokers and 31.3 times more in heavy smokers than in nonsmokers. Surface iron has been shown to increase the inflammatory response to silica in rat lung over that with silica alone (*109–112*).

Lin et al. (*182*) studied obstructive lung disorder in 6726 people in the National Health Assessment Nutrition Examination Survey (III) published by the United States Centers for Disease Control and Prevention, after exclusions for various conditions. The adjusted odds ratio was approximately 1.9 for an increased prevalence of obstructive lung disorder among people in the lowest zinc-intake tertile versus those in the highest tertile, regardless of smoking status. The authors reported relative mean odds ratios for obstructive lung disease of 1.00 for people who had never smoked, 2.60 and 3.37 for former smokers and 4.38 and 7.66 for active smokers in two regression models. After adjustment for creatinine-corrected urine cadmium concentration, the effect of smoking on the risk for lung disorder decreased considerably, suggesting that the cadmium intake from the smoke and not necessarily smoking status itself was a major risk factor for obstructive lung disorder.

Using X-ray microanalysis, Terzakis (*183*) identified particulate compounds in peripheral lung obtained at autopsy from two nonsmokers and one cigar smoker and compared the results with those for 15 people with peripheral lung carcinoma, 10 of whom were smokers. All 15 cancer cases were associated with fibrosis. None of the patients had been exposed occupationally, and none had asbestos bodies in the lung tissue examined. The cancer cases had more carbonaceous pigment in fibrotic tissue vicinal to tumours and more particulate material than the autopsy samples. The particulate material contained silicon, aluminium, phosphorus, vanadium, chromium, iron, nickel, copper, arsenic, cadmium and lead. In all samples examined, silicon was the main element in particles. Silicates in forms consistent with kaolinite, feldspar, talc, muscovite and silica were described.

Although Lynn et al. (*158*), Choux et al. (*159*), Brody and Craighead (*160*) and Heckman and Lehman (*161*), cited above, described extensive aluminium silicate inclusions in alveolar macrophages of smokers, Becker et al. (*184*) found that neutrophils have a stronger oxidative response to silicate than alveolar macrophages, which have a stronger response to oil fly ash particulate (higher in transition metals, lower in silicate, consistent with the data of Sanders et al. [*180*]). They suggested that the wide variation in macrophage response to metal oxides and silica is due to particle composition and concluded that oxidant activation as a consequence of particulate matter is cell specific and that inflamed lung is more susceptible to harm from a broader range of particulate size and composition because of the oxidant stress.

Both airway epithelial cells and alveolar macrophages can phagocytize irritant particles and, as a result, synthesize pro-inflammatory cytokines that induce airway inflammation and consequently contribute to airway lesions in asthma and chronic obstructive pulmonary disorder (*185*). Goto et al. (*186*) showed that alveolar macrophages release macrophage colony-stimulating factor, macrophage inflammatory protein-1β, GM-CSF, IL-6, TNF-α, IL-1β, IL-8 and monocyte chemotactic protein in response to PM_{10}

particulate. Monocytes, which can differentiate into macrophages or dendritic cells, are the main inflammatory cells recruited from bone marrow to the alveoli after exposure to particulate matter, especially that with high metal concentrations.

Beamer and Holian (*187*) found that large numbers of granulocytes were recruited to the lungs of C57BL6 mice in response to exposure to silica, consistent with the findings of Becker et al. (*184*). They also found that the alveolar macrophage-to-dendritic cell ratio was noticeably altered in favour of dendritic cells in comparison with unexposed mice, although a subset of inflammatory CD11b^{high} alveolar macrophages appeared. Beamer and Holian (*187*) suggested that silica-induced apoptosis of alveolar macrophages was one explanation for their decrease in number with time after exposure. The appearance of a new phenotype, and other data, suggested recruitment of this population from peripheral sources. Both alveolar macrophages and dendritic cells may act as antigen-presenting cells. In response to silica exposure, some macrophages and dendritic cells migrated to the interstitium, but only the dendritic cells increased the numbers of CD3$^+$ and CD4$^+$ lymphocytes, suggesting that these cells are the major antigen-presenting cells in this case. Although tobacco smoke transports silicates to the lungs, smoke decreases the number of mouse dendritic cells in the lungs (*188*). Migration of dendritic cells to the interstitium (*187*) may explain their decreased number. Robbins et al. (*188*), however, showed that cigarette smoke compromised antiviral immune responsiveness, perhaps as a consequence of preoccupation of both alveolar macrophages and dendritic cells with inflammatory response and adaptive immunity to the insult from the plethora of tobacco smoke constituents, including metals and silicates.

The TNF-α and IL-1β signals induced by exposure to tobacco smoke, particulate and metals themselves are also indirectly involved in stimulating the fibrotic response to inflammation. TNF-α stimulates production of TGF-β1, which in turn increases the production of connective tissue growth factor, both of which are major stimulators of collagen production (*189,190*). IL-1β increases expression of platelet-derived growth factor-AA and its α receptor on lung fibroblasts. This hormone system is in turn involved in metal-induced airway fibrosis (*191*).

Inflammation, sensitization and pulmonary disease

The prevalence of asthma is increasing worldwide (*192*). Second-hand tobacco smoke has been associated with the development of asthma in children (*119,193,194*). Gavet and Koren (*195*) reported that environmental airborne particulate matter promotes allergic sensitization and increases allergic inflammation and airway hyperresponsiveness. They also reported that exposure of human volunteers to emission source particulate matter samples with high concentrations of iron, nickel and vanadium increased the indices of pulmonary oxidant formation, which in turn correlated with the quantity of transition metals in the samples. Particulate samples with high concentrations of transition metals appeared to be most active in promoting sensitization and exacerbating existing asthma, and they concluded that samples with high concentrations of transition metals enhance sensitization, promote the formation of reactive oxygen species and cause subsequent lung injury, inflammation and airway hyperresponsiveness, leading to airflow limitation and symptoms of asthma. Mutti et al. (*36*) further reported that the median nickel concentrations in exhaled breath condensate were higher in people with asthma than in controls and higher even than in smokers without COPD. Therefore, some of the same transition metals in tobacco smoke particulate may play a role in sensitization. Metal sensitization must thus be considered one of the mechanisms by which atopic asthma and possibly COPD (described as chronic bronchitis, chronic asthma and emphysema) are initiated and progress, with other sensitizing compounds such as polycyclic aromatic hydrocarbons.

Willers et al. (*193*) investigated associations between exposure to environmental tobacco smoke, 'heavy metals' and nicotine (as the urinary metabolite, cotinine) in the households of 23 children with asthma. They found strong associations between the data-based tobacco smoke exposure index and urinary cotinine, indicating inhalation of second-hand smoke. Strong associations were also found between these parameters and nicotine in house dust. Urinary cadmium correlated well with urinary cotinine, as did lead, although the correlation between cotinine and lead was not statistically significant. The authors concluded that the children with asthma were being exposed to 'heavy metals' in sidestream smoke. In a report by the United States Environmental Protection Agency, 2% of the PM_{10} values and 17% of the $PM_{2.5}$ values exceeded the proposed national ambient air quality standards (*196*). The most important contributor to the high levels of indoor particulate matter was environmental tobacco smoke. Each cigarette smoked was estimated to contribute approximately 1 μg/m^3 of airborne particulate matter.

Leikauff (*119*) reported that complex mixtures, including fine particulate matter and tobacco smoke, are associated with respiratory symptoms and hospital admissions for asthma. The hazardous air pollutant components of particulate matter were reported to include 'occupational asthmagens' or components that act as adjuncts during sensitization. Once sensitized, a person may respond to remarkably low concentrations of such compounds. Irritants may also lower the bronchoconstrictive threshold. Of the 33 hazardous air pollutants of greatest concern for exposure in Environmental Protection

Agency reports were compounds of cadmium, chromium, manganese and nickel described as 'suspected of inducing or exacerbating asthma'. Cobalt compounds were also listed as hazardous air pollutants that can exacerbate or induce asthma, although they were not on the list of compounds of greatest concern. Metallic mercury and mercury compounds were included on the list because of their toxicity but were described as respiratory tract irritants that may exacerbate rather than induce asthma.

The prevalence of COPD is increasing worldwide, and it is estimated that it will rise from the fourth leading cause of death in 2004 to the third leading cause by 2030 (*197*). Like atopic asthma, allergic sensitization is often associated with COPD. Itabashi et al. (*198*) showed that, although allergen skin test scores were higher in patients with asthma than in those with COPD, serum immunoglobulin E was significantly higher in elderly patients with COPD or asthma than in healthy people. Although asthma is a distinct disease from COPD, some patients with asthma develop irreversible airway obstruction characteristic of COPD (*199*). Pacheco et al. (*200*) concluded that at least 17.6% of patients who had emphysema associated with smoking had a clear asthmatic profile, consistent with the hypothesis that chronic obstructive diseases have a common origin in underlying sensitization. Silva et al. (*201*) found that active asthma was associated with a mean risk factor of 10 for developing chronic bronchitis, 17 for developing emphysema and 12.5 for 'fulfilling COPD criteria'.

The projected increase in the prevalence of COPD is based mainly on projected increases in tobacco consumption (*197*). As stated above, aluminium, cadmium and lead have been found at higher concentrations in the exhaled breath condensate of patients with COPD than that of nonsmoking healthy controls and at higher levels in current smokers than nonsmokers. COPD patients who smoked had statistically significantly higher concentrations of several metals in their exhaled breath condensate than ex-smokers and nonsmokers with or without COPD (*36*). The role of metals in sensitization and exacerbation of existing COPD warrants further study, and further investigation of the relations between metals in mainstream and sidestream smoke, their potential for sensitization, consequent development of asthma and COPD and exacerbation of both diseases are needed.

Both asthma and COPD are inflammatory disorders. Feron et al. (*168*) and Mueller (*169*) described the risk for carcinogenesis resulting from chronic inflammation of various epithelial and mucosal tissues. Thus, the roles of metals in sensitization and the inflammatory processes of asthma and COPD and exacerbation of both diseases pose carcinogenic risks beyond the immediate pulmonary pathology.

Several of the metals discussed, especially those that strongly induce inflammation or sensitization, such as beryllium, chromium [VI], cobalt, nickel, silicate and those that are toxic chemical irritants perhaps acting by the production of reactive oxygen species, cause interstitial lung disease after occupational exposure (*136*). The concept of tobacco smoking-related interstitial lung disease (characterized by dyspnoea, restrictive pulmonary function, impaired gas exchange and diffuse lung eosinophilic oedematous infiltrates) is relatively recent (*202*). Although the topic remains controversial, numerous authors have reported the clinical symptoms, underlying pathology and radiological observations related to smoking-related interstitial lung disease. Selman (*203*) listed these disorders as including respiratory bronchiolitis, desquamative interstitial pneumonia and pulmonary Langerhans cell histiocytosis, the symptomology and pathology including dyspnoea, cough, restrictive pulmonary function, bronchiole-centred lesions, interstitial and airspace inflammation and fibrosis extending to the alveoli. Caminati and Harari (*204*) further described smoking-related interstitial lung disease with regard to symptoms, smoking history, radiology and pathology. Attili et al. (*205*) described the radiological pathological manifestations. As metals and silicates in industrial exposures, independently of tobacco smoke, and tobacco smoke containing metals and silicate cause inflammation and sensitization and may cause interstitial lung diseases, it is reasonable to consider that these substances are involved in smoking-related interstitial diseases.

An increasing number of non-cancer lung diseases are associated with smoking. In some cases, the data on causes related to tobacco smoking overlap with those on the same or similar diseases caused by metals alone or in particulate matter, including environmental and tobacco smoke. Chronic inflammatory response may, in turn, increase cancer risk.

Summary

Because of space limitations, only the metals described above are included, because they are considered to be of greatest concern due to their concentrations in tobacco or smoke, their carcinogenicity and other toxic effects. Thallium and bismuth, for example, are neurotoxic but are generally found at far lower concentrations in tobacco than aluminium and lead, which are also neurotoxic.

Toxic metals and metalloids are one of the main categories of carcinogen transported in tobacco smoke. The toxicity of metals in smoke is not limited to carcinogenicity but extends to immunological effects. The immunological toxicity of tobacco smoke manifests itself as pulmonary inflammatory response. Industrial exposures to some metals, even at very low concentrations, causes pulmonary inflammation, and exposure to very low concentrations in environmental particulate also causes pulmonary inflammation. Some metals bioaccumulate in the lung and other tissues. Inhalation of tobacco smoke causes pulmonary inflammation. There is evidence that the metals in tobacco smoke particulate play the same role in causing inflammation as do the metals in environmental particulate.

The immunological toxicity of tobacco smoke manifests itself as sensitization responses. Industrial exposure to some metals, even at very low concentrations, causes pulmonary sensitization, and exposure to very low concentrations of environmental particulate rich in metals causes airway sensitization in some people, who, subsequently, may respond to much lower concentrations of the metal or other particulate components. The metal concentration in particulate has been shown to be a major factor in the response. Inhalation of tobacco smoke causes topic or atopic sensitization in some people. There is evidence that the metals in tobacco smoke particulate play the same role in causing sensitization as do the metals in environmental particulate.

Sensitization responses are not limited to responses to the metals themselves. Some metals, such as aluminium in the form of aluminium oxide or hydroxide, are used as adjuvants in inoculations against certain microbial and viral pathogens. There is evidence that mainstream and sidestream smoke have adjuvant effects in sensitization to common allergens, as do the metals themselves in environmental or tobacco smoke particulate. Enhanced sensitization to allergens, whether to metal allergens or to biological allergens as a consequence of the metal adjuvant effect from smoke, may result in asthma. Sensitization also appears to be a factor in the fibrotic progression observed in COPD.

The type of immunological manifestation of exposure to tobacco smoke inhalation depends to some degree on the susceptibility of a person to topic or atopic sensitization. It also appears to depend on the degree of exposure. Suppression of the immune response, especially to pulmonary pathogens, has been observed as a consequence of heavy smoking.

Toxic metals are available in saliva and are transmitted to oral epithelial tissues when smokeless tobacco is used. Oral contact inflammation is known to be a consequence of smokeless tobacco use. Metal sensitization or toxicity resulting from exposure to metals extracted by saliva from tobacco held close to oral tissues might contribute to the oral stomatitis inflammatory lesions observed as a consequence of smokeless tobacco use. The lesions caused by metals alone and by smokeless tobacco are similar. The concentration and distribution of metallothionein in oral mucosa change with the development of the dysplasia that is characteristically observed with leukoplakia, and the cellular metallothionein concentration and distribution in mucosal layers differ dramatically in non-dysplastic oral mucosa and mucosa with moderate dysplasia. Under inflamed conditions, the oral mucosa apparently acts to protect itself from the binding of toxic metals to metallothionein. This is strong evidence for a role of toxic metals in oral inflammation.

The conclusions in this report are those of the author and do not necessarily represent the official position of the United States of Centers for Disease Control and Prevention or the Agency for Toxic Substances and Disease Registry.

References

1. Fowles J, Dybing E. Application of toxicological risk assessment principles to the chemical constituents of cigarette smoke. *Tobacco Control*, 2003, 12:424–430.
2. Hecht SH. Tobacco smoke carcinogens and lung cancer. *Journal of the National Cancer Institute*, 1999, 91:1194–1210.
3. Richter P et al. Surveillance of moist snuff: total nicotine, moisture, pH, un-ionized nicotine, and tobacco-specific nitrosamines. *Nicotine and Tobacco Research*, 2008, 10:1645–1652.
4. Lawler TS et al. Chemical analysis of domestic oral tobacco products: total nicotine, un-ionized nicotine and tobacco-specific nitrosamines. (2010, in internal CDC review).
5. Obrist D et al. Particulate-phase and gaseous elemental mercury emissions during biomass combustion: controlling factors and correlation with particulate matter emissions. *Environmental Science and Technology*, 2008, 42:721–727.
6. Agency for Toxic Substances and Disease Registry. *Toxicological profile for mercury*. Atlanta, Georgia, 1999:58–72,182–183. http://www.atsdr.cdc.gov/ToxProfiles/tp46.pdf (accessed 3 January 2012).
7. Galazyn-Sidorczuk M, Brzóska M, Moniuszko-Jakoniuk J. Estimation of Polish cigarettes contamination with cadmium and lead, and exposure to these metals via smoking. *Environmental Monitoring and Assessment*, 2008, 137:481–493.
8. Hammond D, O'Connor RJ. Constituents in tobacco and smoke emissions from Canadian cigarettes. *Tobacco Control*, 2008, 17:i24–i31.
9. O'Connor RJ et al. Cigarettes sold in China: design, emissions and metals. *Tobacco Control*, 2010, 19(Suppl 2):i47–i53.
10. Frank R et al. Metal contents and insecticide residues in tobacco soils and cured tobacco leaves collected in southern Ontario. *Tobacco Science*, 1977, 21:74–80.
11. Schwartz RS, Hecking LT. Determination of geographic origin of agricultural products by multivariate analysis of trace element composition. *Journal of Analytical Atomic Spectrometry*, 1991, 6:637–642.

12. Cheng S. Heavy metal pollution in China: origin, pattern and control. *Environmental Science and Pollution Research*, 2003, 10:192–198.
13. Xiao T et al. Naturally occurring thallium: a hidden geoenvironmental hazard? *Environment International*, 2004, 30:501–507.
14. Xiao T et al. Environmental concerns related to high thallium levels in soils and thallium uptake by plants in southwest Guizhou, China. *Science of the Total Environment*, 2004, 318:223–244.
15. Golia EE, Dimirkou A, Mitsios IK. Heavy-metal concentration in tobacco leaves in relation to their available soil fractions. *Communications in Soil Science and Plant Analysis*, 2009, 40:106–120.
16. Adamu CA et al. Residual metal concentrations in soils and leaf accumulations in tobacco a decade following farmland application of municipal sludge. *Environmental Pollution*, 1989, 56:113–126.
17. Bache CA et al. Cadmium and nickel in mainstream particulates of cigarettes containing tobacco grown on a low cadmium soil-sludge mixture. *Journal of Toxicology and Reproductive Health*, 1985, 16:547–552.
18. Bell PF, Mulchi CL, Chaney RL. Microelement concentrations in Maryland air-cured tobacco. *Communications in Soil Science and Plant Analysis*, 1992, 23:1617–1628.
19. Mulchi CL et al. Long term availability of metals in sludge amended acid soils. *Journal of Plant Nutrition*, 1987, 10:149–161.
20. Mulchi CL et al. Residual heavy metal concentrations in sludge-amended coastal plain soils—I. Comparison of extractants. *Communications in Soil Science and Plant Analysis*, 1991, 22: 919–941.
21. Mulchi CL et al. Residual heavy metal concentrations in sludge-amended coastal plain soils—II. Predicting metal concentrations in tobacco from soil test information. *Communications in Soil Science and Plant Analysis*, 1992, 23:1053–1069.
22. Rickert WS, Kaiserman MJ. Levels of lead, cadmium, and mercury in Canadian cigarette tobacco as indicators of environmental change: results of a 21-year study (1968–1988). *Environmental Science and Technology*, 1994, 28:924–927.
23. Qiu J. Phosphate fertilizer warning for China. *Nature News*, 2010; doi:10.1038/news.2010.498 (accessed 3 January 2011).
24. International Agency for Research on Cancer. *Smokeless tobacco and some tobacco-specific* N*-nitrosamines*. Lyon, 2007:26 (IARC Monographs on the Evaluation of Carcinogenic Risks to Humans Vol. 89).
25. Maier RH et al. Trace metal characterization of some standard smokeless tobaccos. *Trace Elements in Medicine*, 1993, 10:48–53.
26. Pappas RS et al. Analysis of toxic metals in commercial moist snuff and Alaska iqmik. *Journal of Analytical Toxicology*, 2008, 32:281–291.

27. Rickert WS et al. Chemical and toxicological characterization of commercial smokeless tobacco products available on the Canadian market. *Regulatory Toxicology and Pharmacology*, 2009, 53:121–133.

28. van Ruth SM et al. Interactions between artificial saliva and 20 aroma compounds in water and oil model systems. *Journal of Agricultural and Food Chemistry*, 2001, 49:2409–2413.

29. Baker RR, Dixon M. The retention of smoke constituents in the human respiratory tract. In: *Abstracts of presentations made at the 2005 CORESTA joint meeting of the smoke science and product technology study groups, Stratford-upon-Avon.* Paris, Centre de Coopération pour les Recherches Scientifiques Relatives au Tabac (Abstract SSPT 36).

30. Baker RR. Product formation mechanisms inside a burning cigarette. *Progress in Energy and Combinatorial Science*, 1981, 7:135–153.

31. Jenkins RW Jr et al. Chemical variability of mainstream smoke as a function of aerodynamic particle size. *Journal of Aerosol Science*, 1979, 10:355–362.

32. Nazaroff WW et al. Predicting regional lung deposition of environmental tobacco smoke particles. *Aerosol Science and Technology*, 1993, 19:243–254.

33. Valente P et al. Exposure to fine and ultrafine particles from secondhand smoke in public places before and after the smoking ban, Italy 2005. *Tobacco Control*, 2007, 16:312–317.

34. Oberdörster G, Oberdörster E, Oberdörster J. Nanotoxicology: an emerging discipline evolving from studies of ultrafine particles. *Environmental Health Perspectives*, 2005, 113:823–839.

35. Pääkö P et al. Cadmium and chromium as markers of smoking in human lung tissue. *Environmental Research*, 1989, 49:197–207.

36. Mutti A et al. Exhaled metallic elements and serum pneumoproteins in asymptomatic smokers and patients with COPD or asthma. *Chest*, 2006, 129:1288–1297.

37. International Agency for Research on Cancer. *Overall evaluations of carcinogenicity: an updating of IARC Monographs Volumes 1 to 42.* Lyon, 1987:89–91 (IARC Monographs on the Evaluation of Carcinogenic Risks to Humans Suppl. 7).

38. Corrin B. Aluminium pneumoconiosis. 2. Effect on rat lung of intratracheal injections of stamped aluminium powders containing different lubricating agents and of a granular aluminium powder. *British Journal of Industrial Medicine*, 1963, 20:268–276.

39. Chen WJ, Monnat R, Chen M. Aluminum induced pulmonary granulomatosis. *Human Pathology*, 1978, 9:705–711.

40. Jederlinic PJ et al. Pulmonary fibrosis in aluminum oxide workers. *American Review of Respiratory Disease*, 1990, 142:1179–1184.

41. Burge PS, Scott JA, McCoach J. Occupational asthma caused by aluminium. *Allergy*, 2000, 55:779–780.
42. Agency for Toxic Substances and Disease Registry. *Toxicological profile for aluminum.* Atlanta, Georgia, 2008:13–117. http://www.atsdr.cdc.gov/ToxProfiles/tp22-c3.pdf (accessed 3 January 2012).
43. Addo MA et al. Mineral profile of Ghanaian dried tobacco leaves and local snuff: a comparative study. *Journal of Radioanalytical and Nuclear Chemistry*, 2008, 277:517–524.
44. Shaikh AN et al. Determination of some toxic trace elements in Indian tobacco and its smoke. *Journal of Radioanalytical and Nuclear Chemistry*, 1992, 163:349–353.
45. Dhaware D et al. Determination of toxic metals in Indian smokeless tobacco products. *Scientific World Journal*, 2009, 9:1140–1147.
46. Verma S, Yadav S, Singh I. Trace metal concentration in different Indian tobacco products and related health implications. *Food and Chemical Toxicology*, 2010, 48:2291–2297.
47. Hoffmann D et al. Toxic and carcinogenic agents in moist and dry snuff. *Journal of the National Cancer Institute*, 1987, 79:1281–1286.
48. Kazi TG et al. Determination of toxic elements in different brands of cigarette by atomic absorption spectrometry using ultrasonic assisted acid digestion. *Environmental Monitoring and Assessment*, 2009, 154:155–167.
49. Stephens WE, Calder A, Newton J. Source and health implications of high toxic metal concentrations in illicit tobacco products. *Environmental Science and Technology*, 2005, 39:479–488.
50. Iskander FY, Bauer TL, Klein DE. Determination of 28 elements in American cigarette tobacco by neutron-activation analysis. *Analyst*, 1986, 111:107–109.
51. Swami K, Judd CD, Orsini J. Trace metals analysis of legal and counterfeit cigarette tobacco samples using inductively coupled plasma mass spectrometry and cold vapor atomic absorption spectrometry. *Spectroscopy Letters*, 2009, 42:479–490.
52. International Agency for Research on Cancer. *Overall evaluations of carcinogenicity: an updating of IARC Monographs Volumes 1 to 42.* Lyon, 1987:100–103 (IARC Monographs on the Evaluation of Carcinogenic Risks to Humans Suppl. 7).
53. Agency for Toxic Substances and Disease Registry. Toxicological profile for arsenic. Atlanta, Georgia, 2007:20–375. http://www.atsdr.cdc.gov/ToxProfiles/tp2.pdf (accessed 3 January 2012).
54. Lindberg A-L et al. Impact of smoking and chewing tobacco on arsenic-induced skin lesions. *Environmental Health Perspectives*, 2010, 118:533–538.

55. Counts ME et al. Smoke composition and predicting relationships for international commercial cigarettes smoked with three machine-smoking conditions. *Regulatory Toxicology and Pharmacology*, 2005, 41:185–227.

56. Pappas RS et al. Cadmium, lead, and thallium in mainstream tobacco smoke particulate. *Food and Chemical Toxicology*, 2006, 44:714–723.

57. Doig AT. Baritosis: a benign pneumoconiosis. *Thorax*, 1976, 31:30–39.

58. Agency for Toxic Substances and Disease Registry. Toxicological profile for barium. Atlanta, Georgia, 2007:10,57. http://www.atsdr.cdc.gov/ToxProfiles/tp24.pdf (accessed 3 January 2012).

59. International Agency for Research on Cancer. *Overall evaluations of carcinogenicity to humans*. Lyon, 2009. http://monographs.iarc.fr/ENG/Classification/crthgr01.php (accessed 6 May 2010).

60. Freiman DG, Hardy HL. Beryllium disease: the relation of pulmonary pathology to clinical course and prognosis based on a study of 130 cases from the US Beryllium Case Registry. *Human Pathology*, 1970, 1:25–44.

61. Smith CJ, Livingston AD, Doolittle DJ. An international literature survey of 'IARC Group I carcinogens' reported in mainstream tobacco smoke. *Food and Chemical Toxicology*, 1997, 35:1107–1130.

62. Kelleher PC et al. Beryllium particulate exposure and disease relations in a beryllium machining plant. *Journal of Occupational and Environmental Medicine*, 2001, 43:238–249.

63. Newman LS et al. Beryllium sensitization progresses to chronic beryllium disease. *American Journal of Respiratory and Critical Care Medicine*, 2005, 171:54–60.

64. Reeves AL, Vorwald AJ. Beryllium carcinogenesis II. Pulmonary deposition and clearance of inhaled beryllium sulfate in the rat. *Cancer Research*, 1967, 27:446–451.

65. Rhoads K, Sanders CL. Lung clearance, translocation, and acute toxicity of arsenic, beryllium, cadmium, cobalt, lead, selenium, vanadium, and ytterbium oxides following deposition in rat lung. *Environmental Research*, 1985, 36:359–378.

66. Agency for Toxic Substances and Disease Registry. Toxicological profile for cadmium. Atlanta, Georgia, 2008:43–189. http://www.atsdr.cdc.gov/ToxProfiles/tp5-p.pdf (accessed 3 January 2012).

67. Cekic O. Copper, lead, cadmium and calcium in cataractous lenses. *Ophthalmic Research*, 1998, 30:49–53.

68. Cekic O. Effect of cigarette smoking on copper, lead, and cadmium accumulation in human lens. *British Journal of Ophthalmology*, 1998, 82:186–188.

69. Sulochana KN et al. Chewing of tobacco-leaves, accumulation of cadmium in the lens and cataract. *Investigative Ophthalmology and Visual Science*, 1998, 36:S804.

70. Navas-Acien A et al. Lead, cadmium, smoking, and increased risk of peripheral arterial disease. *Circulation*, 2004, 109:3196–3201.

71. Suwazono Y et al. Biological half-life of cadmium in the urine of inhabitants after cessation of cadmium exposure. *Biomarkers*, 2009, 14:77–81.

72. Paschal DC et al. Exposure of the US population aged 6 years and older to cadmium: 1988–1994. *Archives of Environmental Contamination and Toxicology*, 2000, 38:377–383.

73. Alvarado J, Cristiano R. Determination of cadmium, cobalt, nickel and lead in Venezuelan cigarettes by electrothermal atomic absorption spectrometry. *Journal of Analytical Atomic Spectrometry*, 1993, 8:253–239.

74. Barlas H et al. Heavy metal concentrations of cigarettes in Turkey. *Fresenius Environmental Bulletin*, 2001, 10:80–83.

75. Massadeh AM, Alali FQ, Jaradat QM. Determination of cadmium and lead in different cigarette brands in Jordan. *Environmental Monitoring and Assessment*, 2005, 104:163–170.

76. Lugon-Moulin N et al. Cadmium concentration in tobacco (*Nicotiana tabacum* L.) from different countries and its relationshipwith other elements. *Chemosphere*, 2006, 63:1074-1086.

77. Ogunlewe JO, Osegbe DN. Zinc and cadmium concentrations in indigenous blacks with normal, hypertrophic, and malignant prostate. *Cancer*, 1989, 63:1388–1392.

78. Kazi TG et al. Evaluation of cadmium and zinc in biological samples of tobacco and alcohol user male mouth cancer patients. *Human and Experimental Toxicology*, 2010, 29:221–230.

79. Arora M et al. Association of environmental cadmium exposure with periodontal disease in United States adults. *Environmental Health Perspectives*, 2009, 117:739–744.

80. Schwartz GG, Reis IM. Is cadmium a cause of human pancreatic cancer? *Cancer Epidemiology, Biomarkers and Prevention*, 2000, 9:139–145.

81. Schwartz GG, Il'yasova D, Ivanova A. Urinary cadmium, impaired fasting glucose, and diabetes in the NHANES III. *Diabetes Care*, 2003, 26:468–470.

82. Tsuchiyama F et al. Pulmonary metal distribution in urban dwellers. *International Archives of Occupational and Environmental Health*, 1997, 70:77–84.

83. Mussalo-Rauhama H et al. Cigarettes as a source of some trace and heavy metals and pesticides in man. *Archives of Environmental Health*, 1986, 41:49–55.

84. Hoffmann K et al. The German Environmental Survey 1990/1992 (GerES II): cadmium in blood, urine and hair of adults and children. *Journal of Exposure Analysis and Environmental Epidemiology*, 2000, 10:126–135.

85. Milnerowicz H et al. Effects of exposure to tobacco smoke in pregnancies complicated by oligohydramnios and premature rupture of the membranes. I. Concentration of Cd and Pb in blood and Zn, Cu, Cd and Pb in amniotic fluid. *International Journal of Occupational Medicine and Environmental Health*, 2000, 13:185–193.

86. Shaham J et al. Biological monitoring of exposure to cadmium, a human carcinogen, as a result of active and passive smoking. *Journal of Occupational and Environmental Medicine*, 1996, 38:1220–1227.

87. Becker K et al. German Environmental Survey 1998 (GerES III): environmental pollutants in the urine of the German population. *International Journal of Hygiene and Environmental Health*, 2003, 206:15–24.

88. Pereg D et al. Cigarette smoking during pregnancy: comparison of biomarkers for inclusion in epidemiological studies. *Biomarkers*, 2001, 6:161–173.

89. Snider GL et al. Centrilobular emphysema experimentally induced by cadmium chloride aerosol. *American Review of Respiratory Disease*, 1973, 108:40–48.

90. Pappas RS et al. Cadmium, lead, and thallium in smoke particulate from counterfeit cigarettes compared to authentic US brands. *Food and Chemical Toxicology*, 2007, 45:202–209.

91. Stephens WE, Calder A, Newton J. Source and health implications of high toxic metal concentrations in illicit tobacco products. *Environmental Science and Technology*, 2005, 39:479–488.

92. Moller DR et al. Delayed anaphylactoid reaction in a worker exposed to chromium. *Journal of Allergy and Clinical Immunology*, 1986, 77:451–456.

93. Rüegger M. Lung diseases due to metals. *Schweizerische Medizinizche Wochenschrift*, 1995, 125:467–474.

94. Leroyer C et al. Occupational asthma due to chromium. *Respiration*, 1998, 65:403–405.

95. Hansen MB, Johansen JD, Menné T. Chromium allergy: significance of both Cr(III) and Cr(VI). *Contact Dermatitis*, 2003, 49:206–212.

96. Linneberg A et al. Smoking might be a risk factor for contact allergy. *Journal of Allergy and Clinical Immunology*, 2003, 111:980–984.

97. Sockanathan S, Setterfield J, Wakelin S. Oral lichenoid reaction due to chromate/cobalt in dental prosthesis. *Contact Dermatology*, 2003, 48:342–343.

98. Sógor C, Gáspár A, Posta J. Flame atomic absorption spectrometric determination of total chromium and Cr(VI) in cigarette ash and smoke using flow injection/hydraulic high-pressure sample introduction. *Microchemical Journal*, 1998, 58:251–255.

99. Kim JG et al. Oxidation of chromium(III) to (VI) by manganese oxides. *Soil Science Society of America Journal*, 2002, 66:306–315.

100. Agency for Toxic Substances and Disease Registry. *Toxicological profile for copper*. Atlanta, Georgia, 2004:22–23. http://www.atsdr.cdc.gov/ToxProfiles/tp132-c3.pdf. (accessed 3 January 2012).

101. Massadeh A et al. Simultaneous determination of Cd, Pb, Cu, Zn, and Se in human blood of Jordanian smokers by ICP-OES. *Biological Trace Element Research*, 2010, 133:1–11.

102. Halliwell B, Gutteridge JMC. Oxygen free radicals and iron in relation to biology and medicine: some problems and concepts. *Archives of Biochemistry and Biophysics*, 1986, 246:501–514.

103. Thompson AB et al. Lower respiratory tract iron burden is increased in association with cigarette smoking. *Journal of Laboratory and Clinical Medicine*, 1991, 117:493–499.

104. Wesselius LJ, Nelson ME, Skikne BS. Increased release of ferritin and iron by iron-loaded alveolar macrophages in cigarette smokers. *Journal of Respiratory and Critical Care Medicine*, 1994, 150:690–695.

105. Moreno JJ et al. Release of iron from ferritin by aqueous extracts of cigarette smoke. *Chemical Research in Toxicology*, 1992, 5:116–123.

106. Boyer R, Clark HM, LaRoche AP. Reduction and release of ferritin iron by plant phenolics. *Journal of Inorganic Biochemistry*, 1988, 32:171–181.

107. Ghio AJ et al. Particulate matter in cigarette smoke alters iron homeostasis to produce a biological effect. *American Journal of Respiratory and Critical Care Medicine*, 2008, 178:1130–1138.

108. Padmavathi P, Reddy VD, Varadacharyulu N. Influence of chronic cigarette smoking on serum biochemical profile in male human volunteers. *Journal of Health Science*, 2009, 55:265–270.

109. Ghio AJ et al. Role of surface complexed iron in oxidant generation and lung inflammation induced by silicates. *American Journal of Physiology*, 1992, 263:L511–L518.

110. Ghio AJ, Jaskot RH, Hatch GE. Lung injury after silica instillation is associated with an accumulation of iron in rats. *American Journal of Physiology–Lung Cellular and Molecular Physiology*, 1994, 267:L686–L692.

111. Ghio AJ et al. Lung inflammation after exposure to nonfibrous silicates increases with chelatable [Fe^{3+}]. *Journal of Toxicology and Environmental Health*, 1996, 49:11–28.

112. Castranova V et al. Augmentation of pulmonary reactions to quartz inhalation by trace amounts of iron-containing particles. *Environmental Health Perspectives*, 1997, 105(Suppl.5):1319–1324.

113. International Agency for Research on Cancer. *Inorganic and organic lead compounds*. Lyon, 2006:378 (IARC Monographs on the Evaluation of Carcinogenic Risks to Humans Vol. 87).

114. Agency for Toxic Substances and Disease Registry. *Toxicological profile for lead.* Atlanta, Georgia, 2007:21–169. http://www.atsdr.cdc.gov/ToxProfiles/tp13.pdf. (accessed 3 January 2012).

115. Rhainds M, Levallois P. Effects of maternal cigarette smoking and alcohol consumption on blood lead levels of newborns. *American Journal of Epidemiology*, 1997, 145:250–257.

116. Rhainds M et al. Lead, mercury, and organochlorine compound levels in cord blood in Québec, Canada. *Archives of Environmental Health*, 1999, 54:40–47.

117. Mannino DM et al. Second-hand smoke exposure and blood lead levels in US children. *Epidemiology*, 2003, 14:719–727.

118. Agency for Toxic Substances and Disease Registry. *Toxicological profile for manganese*. Atlanta, Georgia, 2008:38–86. http://www.atsdr.cdc.gov/ToxProfiles/tp151-c3.pdf (accessed 3 January 2012).

119. Leikauff GD. Hazardous air pollutants and asthma. *Environmental Health Perspectives*, 2002, 110(Suppl. 4):505–526.

120. Cotton FA et al. *Advanced inorganic chemistry*. New York: John Wiley and Sons, 1999:758–771.

121. Morsy MA, Khaled MM. Direct electron paramagnetic resonance study of tobacco. 1. Manganese(II) as a marker. *Journal of Agricultural and Food Chemistry*, 2001, 49:683–686.

122. Hakala M et al. Photoinhibition of manganese enzymes: insights into the mechanism of photosystem II photoinhibition. *Journal of Experimental Botany*, 2006, 57:1809–1816.

123. Whittaker, MM et al. The oxidized (3,3) state of manganese catalase. Comparison of enzymes from *Thermus thermophilus* and *Lactobacillus plantarum*. *Biochemistry*, 1999, 38:9126–9136.

124. Murray KJ, Mozafarzadeh ML, Tebo BM. Cr(III) oxidation and Cr toxicity in cultures of the manganese(II)-oxidizing *Pseudomonas putida* strain GB-1. *Geomicrobiology Journal*, 2005, 22:151–159.

125. Matusch A, Depboylu C, Palm C, Wu B, Höglinger GU, Schäfer MK-H, Becker JS. Cerebral bioimaging of Cu, Fe, Zn, and Mn in the MPTP mouse model of Parkinson's disease using laser ablation inductively coupled plasma mass spectrometry (LA-ICP-MS). *Journal of the American Society for Mass Spectrometry*, 2010, 21:161-171.

126. Reaney SH, Bench G, Smith DR. Brain accumulation and toxicity of Mn(II) and Mn(III) exposures. *Toxicological Science*, 2006, 93:114–124.

127. Gomez M et al. Concentrations of some essential elements in the brain of aluminum-exposed rats in relation to the age of exposure. *Archives of Gerontology and Geriatrics*, 1997, 24:287–294.

128. Uz E et al. The relationship between serum trace element changes and visual function in heavy smokers. *Acta Ophthalmologica Scandinavica*, 2003, 81:161–164.

129. Bast-Pettersen R, Ellingsen DG. The Kløve–Matthews static steadiness test compared with the DPD tremor. *NeuroToxicology*, 2005, 26:331–342.

130. Ratcliffe HE, Swanson GM, Fischer LJ. Human exposure to mercury: a critical assessment of the evidence of adverse health effects. *Journal of Toxicology and Environmental Health*, Part A, 1996, 49:221–270.

131. Koch P, Bahmer FA. Oral lesions and symptoms related to metals used in dental restorations: a clinical, allergological, and histologic study. *Journal of the American Academy of Dermatology*, 1999, 41:422–430.

132. Vamnes JS et al. Four years of clinical experience with an adverse reaction unit for dental biomaterials. *Community Dentistry and Oral Epidemiology*, 2004, 32:150–157.

133. International Agency for Research on Cancer. *Overall evaluations of carcinogenicity: an updating of IARC Monographs Volumes 1 to 42*. Lyon, 1987:264–269 (IARC Monographs on the Evaluation of Carcinogenic Risks to Humans Suppl. 7).

134. International Agency for Research on Cancer. *Chlorinated drinking-water; chlorination by-products; some other halogenated compounds; cobalt and cobalt compounds*. Lyon, 1991 (IARC Monographs on the Evaluation of Carcinogenic Risks to Humans Vol. 52).

135. International Agency for Research on Cancer. *Cobalt in hard metals and cobalt sulfate, gallium arsenide, indium phosphide and vanadium pentoxide*. Lyon, 2006 (IARC Monographs on the Evaluation of Carcinogenic Risks to Humans Vol. 86).

136. Kelleher P, Pacheco K, Newman LS. Inorganic dust pneumonias: the metal-related parenchymal disorders. *Environmental Health Perspectives*, 2000, 108(Suppl. 4):685–696.

137. Khamayasi Z, Bergman R, Weltfriend S. Positive patch test reactions to allergens of the dental series and the relation to the clinical presentations. *Contact Dermatitis*, 2006, 55:216–218.

138. Dotterud LK, Smith-Sivertsen T. Allergic contact sensitization in the general adult population: a population-based study from northern Norway. *Contact Dermatitis*, 2007, 56:10–15.

139. Goebeler M et al. Nickel chloride and cobalt chloride, two common contact sensitizers, directly induce expression of intercellular adhesion molecule-1 (ICAM-1), vascular cell adhesion molecule-1 (VCAM-1), and endothelial leukocyte adhesion molecule-1 (ELAM-1) by endothelial cells. *Journal of Investigative Dermatology*, 1993, 100:759–765.

140. Goebeler M et al. Activation of nuclear factor κB and gene expression in human endothelial cells by the common haptens nickel and cobalt. *Journal of Immunology*, 1995, 155:2459–2467.

141. Agency for Toxic Substances and Disease Registry. *Toxicological profile for nickel.* Atlanta, Georgia, 2005:65–75. http://www.atsdr.cdc.gov/ToxProfiles/tp15.pdf (accessed 3 January 2012).

142. Schmidt S et al. Crucial role for human Toll-like receptor 4 in the development of contact allergy to nickel. *Nature Immunology*, 2010, 11:814–820.

143. Dolovich J, Evans SL, Nieboer E. Occupational asthma from nickel sensitivity: I. Human serum albumin in the antigenic determinant. *British Journal of Industrial Medicine*, 1984, 41:51–55.

144. Khater AEM. Polonium-210 budget in cigarettes. *Journal of Environmental Radioactivity*, 2004, 71:33–41.

145. Skwarzec B et al. Inhalation of 210Po and 210Pb from cigarette smoking in Poland. *Journal of Environmental Radioactivity*, 2001, 57:221–230.

146. Desideri D et al. ^{210}Po and ^{210}Pb inhalation by cigarette smoking in Italy. *Health Physics*, 2007, 92:58–63.

147. International Agency for Research on Cancer. *Man-made mineral fibres and radon.* Lyon, 1998:44–46 (IARC Monographs on the Evaluation of Carcinogenic Risks to Humans Vol. 43).

148. Kilthau GF. Cancer risk in relation to radioactivity in tobacco. *Radiologic Technology*, 1996, 67:217–222.

149. Syed U-F, Bari A, Husain L. Leaching of 210Po in human saliva from smokeless tobacco. *Journal of Radioanalytical and Nuclear Chemistry*, 2009, 281:541–546.

150. Peres AC, Hiromoto G. Evaluation of 210Pb and 210Po from cigarette tobacco produced in Brazil. *Journal of Environmental Radioactivity*, 2002, 62:115–119.

151. Papastefanou C. Radiation dose from cigarette tobacco. *Radiation Protection Dosimetry*, 2007, 123:68–73.

152. Savidou A, Kehagia K, Eleftheriadis K. Concentration levels of 210Pb and 210Po in dry tobacco leaves in Greece. *Journal of Environmental Radioactivity*, 2006, 85:94–102.

153. Schayer S et al. 210Po and 210Pb activity in Chinese cigarettes. *Health Physics*, 2009, 96:543–549.

154. Ma JF, Yamaji N. Silicon uptake and accumulation in higher plants. *Trends in Plant Science*, 2006, 11:392–397.

155. Piperno DR et al. Evidence for the control of phytolith formation in *Cucurbita* fruits by the hard rind (Hr) genetic locus: archaeological and ecological implications. *Proceedings of the National Academy of Sciences of the USA*, 2002, 99:10923–10928.

156. International Agency for Research on Cancer. *Silica*. Lyon, 1997:211 (IARC Monographs on the Evaluation of Carcinogenic Risks to Humans Vol. 68).

157. Girod CE, King TE Jr. COPD. A dust-induced disease? *Chest*, 2005, 128:3055–3064.

158. Lynn WS et al. Investigations of black bronchoalveolar human lavage fluid. *Chest*, 1977, 72:483–488.

159. Choux R et al. Inorganic cytoplasmic inclusions in alveolar macrophages. *Archives of Pathology and Laboratory Medicine*, 1978, 102:79–83.

160. Brody AR, Craighead JE. Cytoplasmic inclusions in pulmonary macrophages of cigarette smokers. *Laboratory Investigation*, 1975, 32: 125–132.

161. Heckman CA, Lehman GL. Ultrastructure and distribution of intracellular spicules in rat lung following chronic tobacco smoke exposure. *Journal of the National Cancer Institute*, 1985, 74:647–657.

162. Churg A, Vidal S. Carinal and tubular airway particle concentrations in the large airways of non-smokers in the general population: evidence for a high particle concentration at airway carinas. *Occupational and Environmental Medicine*, 1996, 53:553–558.

163. Rhoades CB Jr, White RT Jr. Mainstream smoke collection by electrostatic precipitation for acid dissolution in a microwave digestion system prior to trace metal determination. *Journal of the AOAC International*, 1997, 80:1320–1331.

164. Amini F et al. In vivo study of metal content of oral mucosa cells in patients with and without fixed orthodontic appliances. *Orthodontic and Craniofacial Research*, 2008, 11:51–56.

165. Kazi TG et al. Interaction of cadmium and zinc in biological samples of smokers and chewing tobacco female mouth cancer patients. *Journal of Hazardous Materials*, 2010, 176:985–991.

166. Davis CC, Squier CA, Lilly GE. Irritant contact stomatitis: a review of the condition. *Journal of Periodontology*, 1998, 69:620–631.

167. Johann ACBR et al. Metallothionein immunoexpression in oral leukoplakia. *Medicina Oral Patología Oral y Cirugía Bucal*, 2008, 13:E156–E160.

168. Feron VJ et al. Health risks associated with nasal toxicants. *Critical Reviews in Toxicolology*, 2001, 31:313–347.

169. Mueller MM. Inflammation in epithelial skin tumours: old stories and new ideas. *European Journal of Cancer*, 2006, 42:735–744.

170. Geiser M et al. Ultrafine particles cross cellular membranes by non-phagocytic mechanisms in lungs and in cultured cells. *Environmental Health Perspectives*, 2005, 113:1555–1560.

171. Ferin J, Oberdörster G. Translocation of particles from pulmonary alveoli into the interstitium. *Journal of Aerosol Medicine*, 1992, 5:179–187.

172. Nielsen GD et al. IgE-mediated sensitisation, rhinitis and asthma from occupational exposures: smoking as a model for airborne adjuvants? *Toxicology*, 2005, 216:87–105.

173. Arnson Y, Shoenfeld Y, Amital H. Effects of tobacco smoke on immunity, inflammation and autoimmunity. *Journal of Autoimmunity*, 2010, 34: J258–J265.

174. Rumold R, Jyrala M, Diaz-Sanchez D. Secondhand smoke induces allergic sensitization in mice. *Journal of Immunology*, 2001, 167:4765–4770.

175. Goel N et al. Effect of smoking on atopic predisposition and sensitisation to allergens. *Indian Journal of Chest Diseases and Allied Sciences*, 2008, 50:329–333.

176. Gilmour MI, Selgrade, MJK, Lambert AL. Enhanced allergic sensitization in animals exposed to particulate air pollution. *Inhalation Toxicology*, 2000, 12(Suppl. 3):373–380.

177. Lambert AL et al. Enhanced allergic sensitization by residual oil fly ash particles is mediated by soluble metal constituents. *Toxicology and Applied Pharmacology*, 2000, 165:84–93.

178. Carter JD et al. Cytokine production by human airway epithelial cells after exposure to an air pollution particle is metal-dependent. *Toxicology and Applied Pharmacology*, 1997, 146:180–188.

179. Schaumann F et al. Metal-rich ambient particles (particulate $matter_{2.5}$) cause airway inflammation in healthy subjects. *American Journal of Respiratory and Critical Care Medicine*, 2004, 170:898–903.

180. Sanders CL et al. Distribution of inhaled metal oxide particles in pulmonary alveoli. *Archives of Internal Medicine*, 1971, 127:1085–1089.

181. Regland B et al. Nickel allergy is found in a majority of women with chronic fatigue syndrome and muscle pain—and may be triggered by cigarette smoke and dietary nickel intake. *Journal of Chronic Fatigue Syndrome*, 2001, 8:57-65.

182. Lin Y-S et al. Cigarette smoking, cadmium exposure, and zinc intake on obstructive lung disorder. *Respiratory Research*, 2010, 11:53–60.

183. Terzakis JA. X-ray microanalysis of peripheral lung carcinomas. *Ultrastructural Pathology*, 1995, 19:167–173.

184. Becker S, Soukup JM, Gallagher JE. Differential particulate air pollution induced oxidant stress in human granulocytes, monocytes and alveolar macrophages. *Toxicology in Vitro*, 2002, 16:209–218.

185. Mills PR, Davies RJ, Devalia JL. Airway epithelial cells, cytokines, and pollutants. *American Journal of Respiratory and Critical Care Medicine*, 1999, 160:S38–S43.

186. Goto Y et al. Particulate matter air pollution stimulates monocyte release from the bone marrow. *American Journal of Respiratory and Critical Care Medicine*, 2004, 170:891–897.

187. Beamer CA, Holian A. Antigen-presenting cell population dynamics during murine silicosis. *American Journal of Respiratory Cell and Molecular Biology*, 2007, 37:29–38.

188. Robbins CS et al. Cigarette smoke decreases pulmonary dendritic cells and impacts antiviral immune responsiveness. *American Journal of Respiratory Cell and Molecular Biology*, 2004, 30:202–211.

189. Sime PJ et al. Transfer of tumor necrosis factor-α to rat lung induces severe pulmonary inflammation and patchy interstitial fibrogenesis with induction of transforming growth factor-β1 and myofibroblasts. *American Journal of Pathology*, 1998, 153:825–832.

190. Bonner JC. Lung fibrotic responses to particle exposure. *Toxicologic Pathology*, 2007, 35:148–153.

191. Lindroos PM et al. Alveolar macrophages stimulated with titanium dioxide, chrysotile asbestos, and residual oil fly ash up-regulate the PDGF receptor-α on lung fibroblasts through an IL-1β-dependent mechanism. *American Journal of Respiratory Cell and Molecular Biology*, 1997, 16:283–292.

192. Buchele G et al. Atopic diseases in childhood and adolescence: worldwide frequencies and trends. A literature review on the International Study on Asthma and Allergies in Childhood (ISAAC). *Allergologie*, 2008, 31:48–55.

193. Willers S, Gerhardsson L, Lundh T. Environmental tobacco smoke (ETS) exposure in children and asthma-relation between lead and cadmium, and cotinine concentrations in urine. *Respiratory Medicine*, 2005, 99:1521–1527.

194. Vork KL, Broadwin RL, Blaisdell RJ. Developing asthma in childhood from exposure to secondhand tobacco smoke: insights from a meta-regression. *Environmental Health Perspectives*, 2007, 115:1394–1400.

195. Gavet SH, Koren HS. The role of particulate matter in exacerbation of atopic asthma. *International Archive of Allergy and Immunology*, 2001, 124:109–112.

196. Breysse PN et al. Indoor exposures to air pollutants and allergens in the homes of asthmatic children in inner-city Baltimore. *Environmental Research*, 2005, 98:167–176.

197. World Health Organization. *World health statistics 2008.* Geneva, 2009. http://www.who.int/whosis/whostat/2008/en/index.html (accessed 2 June 2010).

198. Itabashi S et al. Allergic sensitization in elderly patients with chronic obstructive pulmonary disease. *Respiration*, 1990, 57:384–388.

199. O'Byrne PM, Postma DS. The many faces of airway inflammation—asthma and chronic obstructive pulmonary disease. *American Journal of Respiratory and Critical Care Medicine*, 1999, 159:S41–S63.

200. Pacheco A et al. Caracteristicas asmáticas en pacientes fumadores con enfisema avanzado [Asthmatic characteristics in patients who smoke with advanced emphysema.]. *Archivos de Bronconeumología*, 2003, 39:221–225.

201. Silva GE et al. Asthma as a risk factor for COPD in a longitudinal study. *Chest*, 2004, 126:59–65

202. Rao RN, Goodman LR, Tomashefski JF. Smoking-related interstitial lung disease. *Annals of Diagnostic Pathology*, 2008, 12:445–457.

203. Selman, M. The spectrum of smoking-related interstitial lung disorders: the never-ending story of smoke and disease. *Chest*, 2003, 124: 1185–1187.

204. Caminati A, Harari S. Smoking-related interstitial pneumonias and pulmonary Langerhans cell histiocytosis. *Proceedings of the American Thoracic Society*, 2006, 3:299–306.

205. Attili AK et al. Smoking-related interstitial lung disease: radiologic–clinical–pathologic correlation. *Radiographics*, 2008, 28:1383–1396.